CONQUERING
the Rapids
of Life

CONQUERING
the Rapids
of Life

MAKING *the* MOST *of*
MIDLIFE OPPORTUNITIES

DR. RUTH K. WESTHEIMER
and Pierre A. Lehu

TAYLOR TRADE PUBLISHING
Lanham • New York • Oxford

This Taylor Trade Publishing hardcover edition of *Conquering the Rapids of Life* is an original publication. It is published by arrangement with the authors.

Copyright © 2003 by Dr. Ruth K. Westheimer and Pierre A. Lehu

Published by Taylor Trade Publishing
A Member of the Rowman & Littlefield Publishing Group
4501 Forbes Boulevard, Suite 200
Lanham, Maryland 20706

Distributed by NATIONAL BOOK NETWORK

Library of Congress Cataloging-in-Publication Data

Westheimer, Ruth K. (Ruth Karola), 1928–
    Conquering the rapids of life : making the most of midlife opportunities /
Ruth K. Westheimer with Pierre A. Lehu.
        p. cm.
    Includes index.
    ISBN 1-58979-012-X (hardcover : alk. paper)
    1. Middle age. 2. Midlife crisis. 3. Middle age—Health aspects. 4. Middle
aged persons—Family relationships. 5. Change (Psychology). I. Title: Midlife
opportunities. II. Lehu, Pierre A. III. Title.

HQ1059.4 .W47 2003
305.5'5—dc21   2003000622

♾️TM The paper used in this publication meets the minimum requirements of
American National Standard for Information Sciences—Permanence of Paper
for Printed Library Materials, ANSI/NISO Z39.48-1992.
Manufactured in the United States of America.

I dedicate this book to my late husband, Fred, who took so much pride in my accomplishments and our family: Miriam Westheimer, Ed.D. and Joel Einleger, M.B.A.; Joel Westheimer, Ph.D. and Barbara Leckie, Ph.D.; and the greatest grandchildren on Earth, Ari, Leora, Michal, and Benjamin.

Rabbi Yehuda ben Tema taught: At forty, one reaches the age of understanding; at fifty, the age of offering counsel; sixty is the beginning of older age; at seventy, one earns respect for having the bearing of wisdom; at eighty, one is recognized for having strength and determination. (*Ethics of the Fathers*, Chapter 5, Mishnah 23).

Contents

CONTENTS

Acknowledgments

THE FIRST PERSON I MUST THANK ON BEHALF OF this book is my good friend Dr. David Best, who served admirably as a "matchmaker." Next is Haya Taitel from Ortho-McNeil, without whom this book might never have been born. Then comes Dr. Robert Krasner, who so generously donated his expertise and commuting time. And of course I want to thank my "Minister of Communications," Pierre Lehu, for collaborating with me on this, our tenth book.

Fortunately my list of people to thank for making every new day even better than the one before grows with each book, and I would need an entire chapter to mention them all. Since I'm not allotted that much space, let me just say to all of you, "Thank you, thank you, thank you," and to all of the relatives, cousins, and their families, they also get a hug! There are some, however, that I must mention by name: Ruth Bachrach, Rabbi Stephen Berkowitz, Carlita de Chavez, Marcie Citron, Hersh Cohen, Esther Coopersmith, Martin Englisher, Gabe Erem, Elliot Horowitz, Fred Howard, John Jacobs, Richard Kandel, Alfred Kaplan, Steve Kaplan, Ph.D., Michael and Ronnie Kassan, Bonnie Kaye, Richard and Barbara Kendall, Dr. Harold and Linda Koplewitz, Marga and Bill Kunreuther, Steve Lassonde,

Ph.D., Rabbi and Mrs. William Lebeau, Cantor and Mrs. Michael Kruk, Lou Lieberman, Ph.D., Mary Cuadrado, Ph.D., John and Ginger Lollos, Sandy Lopater, Ph.D., Jonathan and Ruchy Mark, Dale Ordes, Bobby and Vicky Nachamie, Henry and Sydelle Ostberg, Robert Pinto, Fred and Ann Rosenberg, Cliff and Eleanor Rubin, Jeff and Karen Saull, Simeon and Rose Schreiber, Daniel Schwartz, Joanne Seminara, Esq., Romie and Blanche Shapiro, Amir Shaviv, John Silberman, Esq., Jerry Singerman, Ph.D., John and Marianne Slade, Dr. William Sledge, Richard Stein, Hannah Strauss, Jeff Tabak, Esq., Malcolm Thomson, Gary Tinterow, Greg Willenborg, Ben Yagoda, and Froma Zeitlin, Ph.D.

A very special bravo, thank you, and gratitude to the superb professionals at Taylor Trade Publishing, starting with Jed Lyons, followed by Michael Dorr, Ginger Strader, Ross Plotkin, Melaina Balbo-Phipps, and Mary Bearden.

—RKW

Though it's true that in the past twenty-two years Dr. Ruth Westheimer has been a wonderful person to collaborate with, her main job is to make me laugh at least once a day, a duty she has performed with diligence, perseverance, and great skill, and for which I thank her profusely. I also would like to thank my wife, Joanne Seminara, not only for buying me a kayak, but also for climbing into hers to continually test the political waters; my children, Peter and Gabrielle, for helping me to wear all these gray hairs with pride and joy; my mother, Annette Lehu, for steering me in the right direction; and all the members of the vast Seminara clan, which is growing with a rapidity that at times leaves me breathless. Thanks to Merle Frimark and Teresa Jusino for their daily turns at paddling. And a special thanks to all those who have helped to navigate this book through its own set of rapids, most especially Michael Dorr and Ginger Strader.

—PAL

Introduction

IT HAS BEEN HAPPENING SINCE THE DAYS OF ADAM and Eve. Two people meet, fall in love, and before you know it, their lives, which were like two separate rivulets, merge into a romantic babbling brook, with beams of sunlight dancing on its surface and waving wildflowers decorating its banks. As more time elapses, a minimum of nine months, some minnows may appear, swimming along its shoals, and as the years pass, the brook gradually widens out to become a slow-moving river. Going down that river is like riding a large, flat-bottomed raft. There are some ups and downs during the occasional storm, but basically the waters are calm, and every day seems much like the day before.

It would be great if this stage of life could go on forever, with your body never changing and your children tucked safely under your wing; but destiny has other plans. Around some bend, and there's no telling which one, you'll enter a gorge. As the sides of the canyon get narrower, the calm waters will get rougher, and in some places you'll actually be navigating some roaring rapids. This is no time to be riding on a raft, which will get caught up on the rocks and break into small pieces. You need to pull over toward the shore and exchange that raft for a kayak, a lithe craft that can help you navigate what I've labeled "The Whitewater Years."

Many people are afraid of change. If they could actually get their way and keep their lives free of change forever, this fear might be inconsequential. But change, as we all know, is inevitable. You might be able to color those first few gray hairs or flatten out a few of the wrinkles, but no matter how hard you drag at Father Time's feet, they're going to keep marching right along. Your children are going to leave the nest. Your body will undergo some alterations. Your love life will need some attending to. Your job may become less secure. Since all these changes are inevitable, the secret to having a vibrant, interesting, and enjoyable life once you've entered that gorge is not to quiver in fear, but to figure out how to embrace this new lifestyle and make the most of it. Many clouds do have silver linings, but they can be fleeting, and if you're not ready for them, they can pass you right by. So that's the purpose of this book, to teach you how to grab hold of those silver linings and make the most of them.

At this stage you might be saying to yourself, Okay, Dr. Ruth knows everything there is to know about sex, and some of these changes might involve my sex life, but what about the rest of them? Can she really prepare me for these so-called Whitewater Years?

If you were in one of my classes, I'd give you a gold star for asking a very good question. For the answer I have to take you back to when I was entering my Whitewater Years. It was 1980 and I was fifty-two. I was a little college professor and sex therapist. I was Dr. Ruth Westheimer; nobody ever thought to address me as Dr. Ruth. The world beyond my family and friends was unaware of my existence. But then opportunity knocked. I promptly answered and a few years later I was on the cover of *People* magazine, a publication that a short time before I had never even glanced at.

I realize that everybody can't make quite the same leap that I did, but opportunity will knock on everyone's door, that I guarantee. I think that my experience qualifies me as an expert at answering that knock, and I am quite certain that I can help you to make the most of the opportunities presented to you, too. I'm going to give you some solid advice on how to maximize the potential of the rest of your life, especially on how to manage these changes as a couple, because that can be the most difficult part of all of this.

During the years you've been together, you've settled into certain habits that are familiar and acceptable. But when you hit the Whitewater Years and you both start changing in different ways, readapting to the new "you's" is going to be difficult. Your expectations will run into some potholes that will shake that relationship. Now many couples press on with their relationship, despite these changes, but not necessarily with great joy or satisfaction. They snap and bite at each other, unhappy with the way things have turned out. Maybe they were already unhappy before their Whitewater Years, but the children were enough of a distraction for them not to notice how badly their relationship had frayed. But once those children have departed and they're faced with staring at only each other over the dinner table every night, then this new reality may be hard to digest. But it doesn't have to be that way, and together we're going to see how to adapt in such a way that your relationship improves rather than deteriorates.

By the way, there's nothing magic in any of this. This book is not like one of those weight-loss programs that promises to allow you to lose pounds while eating all you want, which can't possibly work. In fact, the advice I'm going to give you is very similar to the type of advice I give in my private practice to people who come to me with some sort of difficulty with their sexual or married life. I'm a behavioral therapist.

I don't get into long, drawn-out therapy where I need to know the entire history of the people who come to see me. I do short-term work designed to make specific improvements in a person's or a couple's love life, and usually it works.

The key step to this process is the first one, admitting the problem. If you don't admit to having a problem, and many people refuse to even talk about sex with their spouses, no less try to fix any difficulties they may be having, then there isn't a chance in the world that you're ever going to make any improvements in your sex life. The same exact thing applies to the changes that occur during the Whitewater Years. If you won't admit that you've undergone some changes, then how are you going to make the necessary adaptations? The answer is, you won't.

A big part of the problem is that despite all the media attention paid to the sexual revolution, there is a lot of basic Puritanism that remains in our lives. There are many subjects that remain taboo. For example, if your eyes change and you need new glasses, you aren't the least bit ashamed to tell people that you have an appointment with the eye doctor. But if your bladder starts acting up and you have to go to the toilet two or three times as often as you did before, you might very well pretend that nothing is amiss and never make an appointment with a doctor to see if something can be done about it. Why? Because it involves your genital area, which is connected to sex, and it causes you to feel ashamed. When you think about it, this is a ridiculous attitude. Why should you suffer from one symptom of aging, a weak bladder, and not with another, weak eyesight? The obvious answer is that no one should, and yet millions do.

So admitting that a problem exists is the first and most important step in arriving at a solution. It is also very important to prepare for these potential problems. Most people have made some provisions for their financial future.

How many people have thought about what their relationship is going to be like five, ten, or twenty years from now? Almost nobody, and yet empty-nest syndrome, which you may have heard about and which I will discuss in great detail later in this book, is best handled long before it arrives.

Many of the problems we humans face as we advance in years may not be totally preventable, but their effects can be mitigated if we prepare properly. For example, people who are overweight tend to develop certain illnesses later in life, like high blood pressure and diabetes. Being a bit overweight at thirty is mostly an issue of appearance. If you're forty and overweight, those potential diseases should be uppermost in your mind. You should be able to use them to motivate yourself to exercise more, as a sedentary lifestyle is even more devastating than having some extra poundage. But if you wear blinders and refuse to accept the fact that you must begin making some changes in order not to suffer from these diseases later on, then there's a good chance that you will have to deal with them.

So alerting you to potential problems is an important role of this book. I'll offer some advice, but if this advice isn't sufficient—and it may not be—at the very least I want you to admit to yourself that you may be facing certain problems, so that you can then go off and get more information, and potentially receive actual treatment for these problems.

You know some of these issues are like a tiny pebble in a shoe. Until you take your shoe off and dump that pebble out, even the tiniest stone can make walking absolutely miserable. Let me return to the bladder example. If all that is needed to lessen your need to run to the toilet is a small pill taken once a day, isn't that worth the trouble of going to the doctor and getting help? So don't accept all of life's little annoyances without putting up at least some sort of fight. We're given so little time on this earth that it's important not to waste even a few moments, and certainly not to allow an entire stage of one's life to be far below its potential level of satisfaction.

While those under twenty-one are always trying to rush the clock, eagerly awaiting every birthday, those over thirty often prefer not to remember that one day a year when their age officially moves forward a notch. There was a time when reaching a certain age meant you received added respect, but that's not true in this society that worships the young instead of venerating the old. Since no one looks forward to entering an age bracket that is widely discriminated against, a great many people of a certain age live in a state of denial. Rather than admit that there have been changes in their lives caused by the passage of time, they prefer to pretend that they're not as old as they are.

First let me say that I believe that no one should allow his or her age to act as a barrier to just about any activity. I'm seventy-four years old and I still go skiing. I have restored the sex life to clients of mine who were well into their eighties. The mistake that people make, and that I'm trying to prevent with this book, is to forgo certain activities but pretend it has nothing to do with their age. There are many couples who once had a satisfying sex life that has since disappeared. Whether they're in their fifties, sixties, seventies, eighties, or even nineties, that shouldn't happen. But for any couple that has hit certain obstacles to having terrific sex, the only way they can get over those obstacles is to admit them and then take appropriate action.

Here's an example. There are women who develop a condition called interstitial cystitis, and as a result, intercourse becomes painful. Rather than go to their gynecologist and say, "I have pain when I have sex," they stop having sex. It's the ostrich burying its head in the sand syndrome. If these women went to the doctor, they'd discover that there are medicines that would alleviate the condition and they could once again enjoy intercourse. But they come to the erroneous conclusion that they've reached some age at which sex is no longer to be a part of their lives and they just stop. They'll still dye their hair, do their nails, wear the latest fashions, and do whatever is necessary to hide their age from society at large, but they mistakenly believe that a change inside their bodies is beyond repair. Or they're too ashamed to speak to their doctor about their sex life. Whatever the cause, they give up one of life's great joys.

I'm here to say loud and clear, don't give up. Accept the fact that you're undergoing some changes, learn what adjustments are necessary, and then learn how to use those adjustments to make life as rich and full as possible.

CHAPTER I

The Whitewater Years Defined

IN MY INTRODUCTION, I STATED THAT EVERY person, and particularly every couple, is going to enter a new phase of his or her life; most likely when the husband and wife reach their fifties, there will be a variety of changes. I labeled this phase the Whitewater Years. This seems contrary to the expectations of most people, especially young adults. When young adults look at their parents' generation, they're seeing a group that is heading for bed when they're first heading out the door to begin partying. From their perspective, it doesn't seem possible that this older generation's lives could be anything like churning rapids. These young people, when thinking about their futures, are more afraid of dying of boredom than being rocketed about by whitewater. And while their parents should know better, many people on the threshold of these years are blithely unaware of what awaits them.

Hidden Dangers

Why aren't the Whitewater Years more apparent? One reason is that they take place over a relatively short period. It's comparable to the period that teens go through when so much about their lives seems confusing as their bodies are changing, especially their hormones. Eventually this period passes and they settle down. The lives of older adults faced with a rash of sudden changes will also calm down, but whether the new calm period is one that brings satisfaction or leaves them miserable is the critical issue. Hopefully this book will give you the proper guidance so that you can create for yourself a life that will bring you as much joy and pleasure as possible.

Another reason you can't tell when a couple is in the Whitewater Years is that much of the turbulence is of an internal nature, and, more often than not, kept secret, especially from those who are younger. Parents don't talk about their sex lives with their children, even less so if things aren't going quite right. Nor do parents want to worry their offspring about their health or their financial problems. They know that young people should be concerned with building their own futures, and so parents will do the best they can to muddle through the Whitewater Years without showing any signs of strain. And, finally, with the media giving so much attention to the young, many adults hitting their fifties and sixties don't want to admit to the world, or even to themselves, that they're getting "old." And so not only do they keep any problems they may be having hidden from their children, but from their friends, neighbors, and co-workers as well.

Of course *old* has become a relative term. With the advances of modern medicine, there are people in their eighties and nineties who are leading vibrant, active lives. So it is natural that someone in their fifties or sixties wouldn't want to be categorized as old. But while the word *old* may not apply, people in these age brackets are undergoing a series of changes that can't be denied. And while it may be natural to want to hide these changes, just because they aren't visible doesn't make them any less turbulent. In fact, the reverse may be true.

Have you ever ridden on the ride in the Disney theme parks called Space Mountain? It's a roller coaster that many find gives them quite a thrill despite the fact that it's not one of those roller coasters with the steepest descents or that pushes riders the furthest back into their seats with its speed. What differentiates Space Mountain from other roller coasters, and gives it its own special zing, is that it is a covered roller coaster and riders zip along the tracks in the dark. You can't see the next descent or turn. Each change in direction takes you completely by surprise, and that's what gives you that gut-wrenching feeling. I'm sure if you were to ride Space Mountain when all the lights were turned on, you'd find it a pretty tame roller coaster compared to many others. But in the dark, it can be quite a scary adventure.

The Whitewater Years are just like Space Mountain. They are like an internal roller coaster that is not visible to those around you. Oh sure, a woman going through menopause may exhibit hot flashes, but the exterior symptoms are of little concern compared to the feelings she's undergoing inside her head. She's facing myriad worries about these physical changes. She's depressed that she's no longer young enough to have children. She's bothered by the fact that her vagina doesn't lubricate as much as it used to. She's concerned because she's becoming more forgetful. Her moods go up and down in ways she's never experienced before. Believe me, she's on quite a ride, though outsiders can only see occasional red flashes of it.

Roller coasters are not everyone's cup of tea, and so most people never once climb aboard one. And even if you love them, the ride lasts only a few minutes and has no lasting consequences. The Whitewater Years, on the other hand, are not a ride that you can skip, and when you're done, you'll find changes that will last forever. So here's a case where you want to turn the lights on, not because you want your offspring to see you thrown about, but so you can prepare yourself for each upcoming twist and turn because how well you adjust to them will affect the rest of your life. So don't play ostrich and hide your head in the sand, but instead read on, because by facing these changes, you'll find them a lot less bothersome.

Think Positive

And don't forget that people who go on roller coasters do so because they're out for a good time, even if their insides do churn like crazy as they're waiting in line to board and then go off the charts as they whiz about in one of those speeding gravity machines. And the same is true for all those who go out of their way to find rivers that have whitewater for the thrill of negotiating rapids in a small boat. So while you will certainly be encountering some turbulence as you go through this period, if your attitude is right, you may find yourself enjoying at least parts of it. You'll discover the joys of having privacy again. You'll find that removing the worries of an unintended pregnancy enhances sex. You can have a few too many drinks without worrying what the kids will think. You can use the telephone at home. You can curse like a trooper without setting a bad example. You can have friends over on a school night. Etc., etc. So the Whitewater Years aren't all bad; they're just a bit bumpy.

The Sandwich Generation

By the way, the pressure of the Whitewater Years isn't unidirectional. Having your children leave home changes your life, but so does having parents who are becoming truly old. Some people in their eighties or nineties can remain self-reliant right up until the day they pass away. Others, sadly, develop a variety of illnesses, which means they need a lot more care. And as their children, at least part of that duty may fall on your shoulders. (And with two sets of parents to deal with, the odds obviously increase that such a burden will befall you as a couple.)

Since it's impossible to predict what type of problems elderly parents may develop, there's no way of telling what kinds of extra pressure this will eventually put on your own relationship. In some cases it will be minimal, while in others an elderly parent who needs lots of attention and care may have to live under your roof. I'll have some advice on how to handle such situations later in this book.

Other Health Issues

In addition to the expected problems arising from aging, like menopause, one or both of you may experience other health issues that can also impact your relationship. A serious health problem will certainly add to your level of stress, but even minor afflictions can be annoying, especially if they linger or become permanent. Something as simple as a hearing loss can mean that you want the volume of the television set at different levels, which in turn can cause a regular set of squabbles.

While you agreed to stay together in sickness or in health, and should live up to that pact, you also owe it to each other, if not to yourself, to take care of any such health problems as quickly as possible. Again speaking of hearing impairment, many people wait years before going for help, and the person who is most annoyed is the spouse. This is a cause for needless conflict; so if you develop a health problem, go get it taken care of, if not for your own peace of mind, then for that of the person you love. I'll touch more upon this later in the book.

Case History: Geri

All of Geri's friends thought she had an ideal marriage. Anytime Geri and her husband were at a party, they both held court keeping everyone in stitches. What nobody noticed is that, while at the party, they never said two words to each other. And the situation wasn't much better at home. They hadn't had sex in over a year and they rarely shared even a meal. Probably the only reason the word *separation* hadn't come up was that there were no conversations taking place in which it could.

The Ideal Couple

I see some married couples in my office, or get letters from others, who say that to their friends, neighbors, and relatives theirs is the perfect marriage, when actually their relationship is in terrible shape and what the world around them sees is all an act. You may even know couples like that, who seemed to have an ideal marriage and then suddenly separate in a vicious divorce. "What happened?" all their friends ask, wondering nervously whether their own marriage might curl up and die from some mysterious disease they didn't know they had.

What happened was that the problems this couple was undergoing were well hidden, maybe even from each other. When they hit their Whitewater Years, the changes that took place increased the pressure, and their already weakened marriage couldn't take it.

The Whitewater Years don't destroy the vast majority of marriages, but they do afflict many with damage, sometimes even severe damage. The couple's sex life is most likely to be wounded. There are two reasons for this. One, some of the changes will have a direct effect on their sex life, necessitating certain compensatory adjustments if their sex life is to continue. But your sex life is a delicate asset and can be damaged by other factors that get thrown at you that have nothing whatsoever to do with sex. For example, if a man feels that his job is on shaky ground, or worse yet, he loses his job, that's going to have a severe impact on his sex life, and therefore his wife's sex life too. If the couple recognizes what is happening, repairs to the couple's sex life can be made, even if it takes a little time, no matter what happens to his career. But if they don't know the cause of their loss of libido, and if they assume it has something to do with their age and is therefore permanent, then it will become permanent. A sexless marriage can continue forever, it's true, but such a marriage is certainly nowhere near as satisfying as one that includes regular lovemaking. And, of course, a sexless marriage is a lot more vulnerable to a potential breakup.

Changes Begin Slowly

Another factor that can serve to mask the Whitewater Years is that some of the effects are spread out over time. A man of twenty who can have a new erection minutes after having had an orgasm may require several hours to get another erection when he's in his thirties, which may become a day or more when he's in his forties and that can stretch to days and even a week as he gets even older.

Another change that occurs is that a man requires physical stimulation to obtain an erection. In other words, he needs foreplay just like his wife always did. I'll get more into this in a later chapter, but I bring it up now because it's easy to see that the wife may interpret this change to mean that he's no longer excited by her. And so slowly, over a matter of years, their sex life decreases to the point where it ceases altogether. Because this takes place over time, they adapt to living in a sexless marriage. Had it happened suddenly, they might have gone for help, but at this point, they decide, again wrongly, that it is a part of the aging process and that there is no recourse.

Menopause is another factor that takes some time to fully play out. Menopause is not considered to have occurred until a woman has not had her period for one full year. But perimenopause, the period before menopause during which women undergo many changes due to ups and downs in the levels of hormones, can last for more than a decade.

"Hold it," I hear you saying, "if these changes can take decades, why the whitewater analogy? Is this a gradual change that I have years to adapt to or not?" Here's the problem. While many of these changes have a beginning phase that starts much earlier, there is a certain period in which their effect takes a more dramatic turn, such as when perimenopause turns into menopause. And then these gradual changes have a multiplying effect when they start to come together. Sure you knew years ahead of time that your children would go off to college, and hopefully you were saving for that eventuality, but when it actually takes place, when they're out of the house and the bills are pouring in, it's going to be a shock. And it's a shock your kids won't see because they'll be gone!

What is true is that the Whitewater Years are different for every couple. For some, many of the factors will occur for each right around the same time, and their Whitewater Years will be quite an adventure, while for other couples, for example those who had a late child who is much younger than the rest of the brood, the changes may be much more spread out and so the waters won't really boil as much. Nevertheless, the changes are unavoidable, and whether their impact is felt over a longer or shorter period of time, they will be felt.

A Cumulative Effect

And no matter how long it takes these changes to come about, it's their cumulative effect that causes the biggest shocks. Those who are having problems with their sex life are going to have a harder time coping with the departure of their children than those who can comfortably cling to each other. When in the same household the woman is going through menopause while the man is discovering that his penis no longer becomes erect as easily as it once did, it's obvious that neither party is going to be able to give the other the required amount of sympathy. They may both end up resenting the other for being callous and their relationship may suffer drastically because of it. Now throw in a bladder problem for the woman, hair loss for the man, the death of a friend for the woman, and a shaky job for the man and you can easily see that the couple can become overwhelmed by all that is happening to them.

Since it is impossible to predict when these pressures might occur, or to avoid them, it may seem like the raging waters of the Whitewater Years might be impossible to navigate. To answer that, let's return to something I said earlier: when entering these rapids, you must get off the clumsy raft and climb into an agile kayak.

9

Leaving the Raft, Climbing into Your Kayak

When you were all together as a family, with all the children at home, kayaks weren't an option. If a storm arose and you encountered some choppy water, you had no choice but to cling to that raft. But since you were expending so much energy worrying about your children, any early effects of the Whitewater Years weren't so apparent. What makes the departure of your children so dangerous to your relationship is that suddenly your focus changes. Your relationship to each other becomes much more important when there are only two of you. Where you might once have avoided fighting in front of the children, small squabbles can suddenly flare into major battles. When you might have been distracted from nitpicking your spouse by the presence of a child, your nitpicking can turn into nagging when you're only two. Each little bad habit or foible becomes magnified and oh so much more annoying. And when you're dissatisfied and fighting about little things, how can you make the repairs to the bigger rents in your relationship?

The Whitewater Years may start slowly, they may drag out over time, but their cumulative effects can eventually reach the point where the stress becomes too much and the relationship collapses. But if you're in your kayaks, deftly avoiding the rocks and falls that are trying to suck you under, then when you come out of the rapids, you can easily tie your kayaks together and peacefully sail for home. Let me give you an example of what I mean.

With the onset of menopause may come mood swings. Add to those mood swings the sadness that can come from having an empty nest, and a woman could become severely depressed. One common result of the blues is that her desire for sex may evaporate. Now if the couple doesn't understand that this situation is temporary, the husband and wife both might lose hope and he might decide to give up on her. He may feel that the marriage isn't worth saving and say to himself, "Let me get off of this raft!"

But if they're both aware that this is a short setback that is soon going to stabilize, they'll be more willing to give each other some space and have the patience to wait until she adapts both to menopause and having her children out of the house. And the very fact that they're each steering their own course will probably speed up the healing process. It may only be a matter of weeks, or at worst a few months, before she's feeling sufficiently back to normal, or at least sufficiently in control, for her to start feeling sexy again.

And what was he doing while she was adjusting to her new life? I'll get into this in greater detail a bit later on, but basically he's paddling away, trying to figure out where he's headed as well. As long as he stays occupied and has faith that their sex life will soon be back to normal, he'll be able to wait out this period.

To once again compare this period to the one teens go through, this is a time when the apron strings must be cut. When people go through change, they have to complete the process on their own before they can reestablish full contact with their partner. They have to find their own way and establish that they can make it on their own as an independent person. That's not to say that you have to split up during this process—far from it. You need to know that there's someone there for you. It's the buddy system, where if you get really stuck, your partner can row over to help you. On the other hand, if you keep your kayaks too close together, you'll end up getting in each other's way.

Case History: Anne and Edward

Anne gave up her job with an insurance company when she had children. Her husband, Edward, had earned a good living, and they decided that it was better to have her stay home so that they could have more children, four, than to have her go back to work. When her kids were in high school, Anne went back to school to learn nursing, and after her youngest left for college, she took a job at a nearby hospital. As the newbie, she was given night assignments, so that she and Edward didn't get to see much of each other. Anne's salary was helpful in paying for the college tuitions, but Edward resented having to eat alone almost every night.

Separation Anxiety

Having lost my immediate family to the Holocaust, I know the feeling of separation anxiety very well. I have a very hard time saying goodbye to loved ones, even if they live close by and I'll be seeing them the next day. Letting your partner go off on his or her own kayak is definitely going to cause you some anxiety. Whether it be to start a new career, go back to school, take up a hobby, make new friends, change eating habits or exercise routines, get up earlier, go to bed later, learn a musical instrument, or learn how to surf the web on a computer, you're going to wonder whether these new aspects of your partner will change or keep him or her from coming back to you. And since you're going to be making some changes too, you will be wondering whether the two new "you's" will be compatible.

If you allow the growth to take place, if you allow your partner to change and yourself to change, assuming the relationship was basically sound to begin with, you will definitely get back together. It's like parents who fought with their teens tooth-and-nail and then find themselves best friends once they become adults. Of course, if your relationship is on shaky ground, then these changes that you go through might cause a reassessment that will end the relationship. But since trying to avoid these changes is impossible, in the long run you'll be better off allowing them to occur. For example, in the case of Anne and Edward, eventually Anne will be able to switch to a day shift, even if it means going to a different hospital, and their life will become more normal. Until then, however, Edward will have to be patient. He has to appreciate that this is something that his wife wants to do and be supportive rather than just look at it as an inconvenience.

Learning to Portage

While I'm telling you to climb into your own boats and seek your own path, you're not supposed to drift too far from each other. The main reason is that in some instances you will need each other's support to get through a particularly bad rough spot. In real life, if you're on a river and encounter rapids that are just too strong, you leave the water and portage your boats, that is to say you carry them downstream to where the river quiets down a bit. While this is obviously a safer way to go, it is also much slower. Since one person may not be able to carry the boat by him- or herself, the two of you would have to carry one boat, and then go back to get the other one and carry it to the point of safety. What this method requires is teamwork and patience. If you are able to work as a team and carry each other over the really rough spots, then the Whitewater Years won't be as harmful. But if you're each so wrapped up in your own troubles that you can't be bothered to give your partner assistance, then you both might get in over your heads.

Developing Patience

Some people go through life apparently not affected by anything. The world could be coming apart at the seams and they wouldn't twitch a face muscle. That's a wonderful attribute, but let's face it, such patience is not a gift that everyone possesses. It's particularly hard to maintain your composure in a world that is so filled with stress. Forgetting the effects of the Whitewater Years, getting through a normal day at work can be enough to drive anyone over the edge. In fact, just commuting to and from work can be an enormous hassle. So while we all have some patience, our supply can easily get stretched thin. That means finding the inner strength to help your spouse get through some rough spots can be a very difficult task if you're going through rough spots of your own.

Here it is time for a confession: I am one of the most impatient people in the entire world. Most of the time, if I want something, I don't like waiting for even one split second. And while I have always been in a hurry, ever since becoming "Dr. Ruth," I can satisfy my urge for immediate gratification a lot more easily than I could before. On the other hand, if I really want something and I have to wait in order to get it, that's what I do—I wait. In other words, despite my notorious impatience, I can also be very patient if need be.

The point I am trying to make is that even if you are always pressed for time, if your entire relationship is at stake, you can, in fact you must, exhibit the required patience. You must learn to take a deep breath and say, "We're going to work this out" instead of "I can't take this for one more second." Let me be very clear, I am not suggesting that you suddenly develop the biblical patience of Job. Under circumstances when you would have normally exhibited impatience, like in a traffic jam, go right ahead and scream out your frustrations. You can't change your entire personality. But if your relationship requires you to exhibit some patience at a particular point of time, then you must take control of your temper and give your spouse the time and effort that he or she requires.

Case History: Ben and Mary

Mary was having a hard time with menopause. She seemed to have hot flashes quite regularly and suffered miserably with them. One night her husband, Ben, came home from work and found her sitting in front of a fan, half undressed, her face beet red. Instead of asking her how she was feeling, he asked what she'd made for dinner. When she told him that it was too hot to cook and so she hadn't made anything, he blew up at her.

Ben was one of those men who has a short fuse when he's hungry. All the way home he was thinking about the delicious meal he was going to find when he walked through the door, and when all he saw was an empty plate, his disappointment quickly turned to anger. But the truth is, anger wasn't going to fill his stomach. The better approach would have been to either order in pizza or Chinese food, or cook something himself. Rather than directing your anger at your partner in a situation like this, aim for the real source of the problem, your hunger, and do something about it. Just having a slice of bread and butter to tide you over might do the trick.

But, of course, Mary didn't help the situation. She didn't say, my hot flashes are making me miserable. She was embarrassed by the tricks her body was playing, and so she simply said it was too hot to cook. Ben's hunger made that excuse seem like a personal affront. So you see, it's important for both parties to communicate to each other what is really going on.

The immediate payoff in a situation like this will be that his hunger will be satisfied much sooner and there won't be any fireworks. But more important are the long-run benefits, assuming that such "random acts of kindness" are repeated regularly. By admitting the real problem, she has opened herself up, furthering the possibility of other conversations of a more intimate nature. For example, if another effect of menopause is that she is not lubricating the way she used to when she becomes sexually aroused, then it is important that she be able to tell her partner that she requires the use of a lubricant. If they've been open about their communications and if he's been understanding of her problems in general, then this shouldn't pose a major difficulty. But if that has not been the case, if she's felt uncomfortable talking to him about any of the symptoms of menopause or he's not given her the comfort she seeks, then to avoid the pain of intercourse without a lubricant, she just may avoid intercourse altogether. And that will weaken the relationship even further.

Ripple Effects

As you can see, there are ripple effects to many of the issues brought about by the Whitewater Years, and many of these end up having a negative impact on the couple's most intimate connection, their sex life. You might think that two people who have been having sex literally for decades would know better than to act in a manner that would be self-destructive to their sex life. But logic doesn't always take command when it comes to sex. When your upbringing, from the time you were a little child, has taught you that sex is something that remains private, in a moment of crisis, your natural instinct is not to be open about sexual matters, but to repress them. On top of that, the libido, the part of you that causes sexual arousal, is very sensitive. If you're angry with your partner for some other reason, having nothing to do with sex, the likelihood is that your libido will sound a retreat and you'll have great difficulties creating or maintaining desire for your partner. But then, if you're not having sex, you'll start to resent your partner for it, and a vicious cycle builds up that takes some very big bites out of the foundation of your relationship.

The Tip of the Iceberg

One reason the Whitewater Years are so treacherous is not just because of the rocks that you do see, but also because of all those you don't but that could still damage your relationship. So if not handled with care, that uncooked dinner caused by a hot flash could cause a chain of events that will put a crimp in your sex life; perhaps even a permanent one. There's no way that you could predict that at the time, and so it would be easy to blunder down this particularly treacherous waterfall. But if you are aware of even potential dangers, as I hope you will be by the time you finish this book, then with a few deft strokes of your paddle, you can sidestep these hidden rocks and continue on safely.

Up to this point, I've been painting a fairly negative picture of the Whitewater Years, much the way roadside signposts warn you of curves, falling rocks, or suicidal deer. But, of course, when the road is smooth and straight, there are no signs, and while there are certainly potholes you want to avoid during the Whitewater Years, there can also be miles

17

and miles of smooth sailing. This is especially true for couples who have been open with each other all along. If you've been talking about your sexual needs since maybe even before you got married, discussing a dry vagina or an obstinate penis won't be that big of a deal. In fact, in terms of your sex life, many couples find a renewal once their children have left and they can enjoy the benefits of complete privacy. Going for romantic dinners or quiet drives in the country becomes a lot easier without children around. Your romance can grow and blossom if the conditions are right. In other words, the post–Whitewater Years can be terrific, and if you've prepared your relationship for the Whitewater parts of your life, even that phase can be relatively trouble-free. If you're reading this book and you're not yet at the Whitewater stage and you're ready to make the commitment to fully prepare yourselves, then I can safely predict that you'll emerge with a stronger relationship than when you started. If you're already in your Whitewater Years, then it will be that much tougher, but with this book to guide you, I trust that the ride will be invigorating but not dangerous.

CHAPTER **2**

Menopause

I OWE A LOT TO MODERN MEDIA; WITHOUT IT, I wouldn't be "Dr. Ruth," internationally known sex therapist, but simply Dr. Ruth Westheimer, college professor with a private practice. And they say that you shouldn't bite the hand that feeds you, but . . . my personal opinion is that altogether too much is made of menopause in this culture.

The short-term effects of menopause exist, there's no doubt about that, and they can certainly be annoying, at their mildest, and maddening, at a more severe level. But they're not life threatening; at least in the short run, many of them fade away on their own and, most important, the more attention you pay to them, the worse they appear to be. So in my opinion, the less fuss you make about going through menopause, the better your overall experience with this unavoidable stage in life will be.

Now part of this opinion is based on my personal philosophy, which is to accentuate the positive, and not only has this worked for me, but I have no doubt that having such an outlook would benefit everyone.

My opinion is also partially based on my personal experience, and I have to admit that there may be women for whom menopause is much worse than what I went through, whatever their attitude. I don't want to minimize their troubles, or pretend that even at its very faintest symptoms, menopause is something you can ignore entirely. A hot flash most certainly makes itself known.

The main thing I want to stress is that whatever level of symptoms you're going to experience, your attitude will play a part in the severity. So while you cannot prevent menopause from occurring, you can control how severe an event this might be in your life.

Of course, I'm speaking on the psychological level. Unless you've lived in some deep valley without any media contact, you also know that there are potential medical treatments that can alleviate the symptoms of menopause. This form of treatment is called hormone replacement therapy (HRT). But that probably means that you also know that these treatments have potential side effects, which may or may not make the treatments themselves too dangerous to consider.

I will consider these treatments a bit further on, but let me say right here that I am not a medical doctor. Not only am I not a medical doctor, but I often go out of my way not to learn about some aspects of medicine. My main reason for adopting this philosophy is that if I filled my head with a smattering of medical knowledge, I might be tempted to pass on some of this information as factual, and if it happened that I got some of it wrong, then I might lead some reader or listener astray. If my ignorance caused them any harm, I would feel terrible, and so I scrupulously avoid giving out medical information. But what's different about a book, as opposed to what can pop out of my mouth, is that an actual medical doctor can look over what I have put down on paper in order to make certain that it is correct. So I'm going to give you a smattering of medical facts in this chapter, and in other parts of the book as well, but rest assured that when you are reading them that it is not just some idle thought of mine, but real medical information carefully gone over by a highly educated doctor.

See a Doctor

No matter how correct the information I pass on to you, it is not the same as hearing it from your doctor. Now I have as healthy a skepticism of doctors as anyone. I've been misdiagnosed several times despite being a celebrity (or maybe because of it, I don't know). But whenever I was in doubt, I didn't ignore the advice I was given; I went for a second opinion. Medical science has gotten more and more sophisticated and as a layperson, it is very, very difficult for you to make a judgment about many medical conditions on your own. My friend Dr. Robert Krasner believes second opinions benefit physician and patient. In the event the second opinion is different, which is rare, the physician can learn from the experience. In most cases, the second agrees with the first, and the patient is more confident in his or her doctor. So I strongly advise you to go to your doctor whenever a health issue arises. After having done so, don't be afraid to ask lots of questions, and then, if you still have doubts, consult another physician. It's your health and you have every right to be as picky as you want.

But as sophisticated as modern medicine is, it's also not an absolutely exact science. Sometimes you just have to accept the fact that there is no one answer, at least not yet. Sometimes it's not a question of black and white, but various shades of gray, and so you're going to have to make a choice without knowing whether your choice is absolutely right or wrong. That's certainly the case with the possible treatments of the symptoms of menopause.

Menopause as a Couple

I know I promised to give you some actual medical information about menopause, and I will, I will, but before I do let me get to issues that are at the heart of why I've written this book, for after all there are plenty of books on menopause that will give you much more medical information than I can give you in one chapter. My expertise is in dealing with people as couples, and how to handle menopause as a couple is absolutely one area that seems to be sorely neglected in all of the literature about this change.

Since only the woman is going through these changes, what, might you ask, does the woman's husband have to do with all of this? The answer is, plenty. I'm going to give you an example that comes from the opposite end of reproduction, but one that I think will illustrate my point. Very often, couples who have spent years unsuccessfully trying to conceive a child find themselves unexpectedly pregnant soon after adopting a child or using some artificial means of insemination. Under these circumstances their inability to conceive was likely to be some sort of stress-related issue, and once that stress disappeared with the arrival of a child, their problems with infertility disappeared.

Similarly, stress can worsen the symptoms of menopause. Now some stress is unavoidable. If you hate your job but it pays well and you wouldn't be able to get another of equal pay and you have lots of expenses, then you could be stuck. But if your stress is on the home front, then with the help of your spouse there are compromises that can be made that could alleviate that source of stress. And by doing that, menopause could seem less of a burden.

Alleviating the stress in a relationship is not something that one partner can do by him- or herself. Each partner must play a role. Sure you could say, "I'm going to ignore his bad habits," but let's face it, if you've never been able to do it before, you're not going to be able to do it when you're even further stressed by the worries of being menopausal.

So in order to lower your level of stress, you're going to have to work as a team. And the first step will be that you're *both* going to have to understand at least the basics of menopause.

How Men Think

One reason for men's lack of understanding is that they adjust to logical situations more easily than emotional ones. They'll spend hours trying to figure out how to make a car engine work better because it's something they can touch and feel and see. When it comes to the human psyche and what makes it tick, since that's such an ephemeral area, men, for the most part, aren't all that interested.

So if your male partner can be made to understand that your problems regarding menopause aren't all in your head but are caused by changing levels of hormones, he'll be more forgiving than if he just lumps what you're going through into "female trouble." That's why an equation like "wife minus hormones equals change" is one that he can accept a lot more easily than this strange word, menopause. (Perhaps if women didn't shut men out from menstruation, they would also be more understanding of menopause, but from the moment of their very first period, girls do their best to hide this aspect of their femininity, and so boys become conditioned to ignore it.)

Case History: Penny and Carl

As Penny entered menopause, she quickly noted that her vagina no longer produced the same amount of lubrication when she was aroused. She knew the cause, but because several of her friends had recently lost their husbands to younger women, she'd been trying her best to keep the fact that she was going through menopause from her husband, Carl. But Carl noticed that she wasn't lubricating anymore and concluded that she was no longer interested in him sexually. Since sex had become somewhat painful to Penny, she didn't seem to mind when Carl stopped initiating sex, not realizing why his level of desire had changed. But as their sex life came to an end, their relationship began to suffer as well.

The Changes He Will See

The other reason that men need to be more knowledgeable about menopause is that one of those changes is going to affect men directly. A postmenopausal woman who is not taking HRT is going to have a much-reduced level of vaginal lubrication. This is not a big deal. All that is needed is to use an artificial lubricant, of which there are many sold over the counter. That should be simple enough, but many couples end up making it complicated because they don't really communicate about this problem.

If he doesn't know that this is a symptom of menopause, he's likely to think that the cessation of lubrication means he's not arousing her anymore. And even some women think that out of ignorance. They wind up convincing themselves that because they're not making as much lubrication as they once did that they are not aroused, when that's not true. What is true is if a person thinks he or she is not aroused, his or her level of arousal will sink like a stone. And so you wind up with sexless marriages caused by nothing more than a lack of information. And if both halves of the couple are uninformed, then the effect will be doubled.

The Flip Side

There can also be a positive side to this. Some couples have been having sex the same way for years so that their love life has become boring. Along comes menopause and a few things change. One, there is no possibility of causing a pregnancy. Whatever form of birth control they were using is no longer necessary. And even more important, whatever worries they had about causing an unintended pregnancy are also gone. That can allow for much more spontaneous sex, and if the house is now empty of children, that can also make spontaneity more feasible, which in turn will give their lovemaking a needed boost.

And the process of adding a lubricant can also stimulate intimacy. Instead of the wife doing this process surreptitiously in the bathroom, the husband should be in charge of it, and I guarantee you that most men are going to enjoy any activity that has them up close and personal with their partner's vagina. And if the woman is still producing some lubrication, some of his saliva may be sufficient to allow for comfortable penetration of his penis, and again, some men enjoy performing cunnilingus.

And there's one more benefit that the male is going to get from increasing the level of intimacy, and that will come into play when down the road, if not already, he needs some more help as well. I'll get into this more in chapter 4, but since he will need some added stimulation, taking charge of his wife's lubrication is a favor to his wife that will stand him in good stead when the time comes for him to ask a favor in return.

Two Heads Are Better Than One

There's one additional reason for keeping your spouse in the loop—two heads are better than one. Anytime you go to see a doctor about some medical condition that is causing you serious symptoms, it is sometimes better to have someone else in the consultation room with you. If your doctor says something to you that causes your emotions to go into overload, your mind might go blank and then you won't hear the rest of what your doctor has to say. Or your head might be too clouded to think of questions that you want answered. Having a loved one with you, who perhaps can write down what the doctor says and who might remain more clearheaded so as to be able to ask questions, can be very important.

Of course this is more vital when you're dealing with a serious condition, like cancer. But even with something as everyday as menopause, your partner might either pick up something the doctor says that doesn't register with you or think of a question you might not have thought about.

So you see, even though only the woman will be experiencing the symptoms of menopause, teamwork can be a key in dealing with those symptoms.

Defining Menopause

So what exactly is menopause? In order to explain it to you, I've been learning a lot myself. For example, did you know that a female fetus of twenty weeks, that is to say one that is still inside the womb, has six million eggs, but by the time she's born she has only two million? And by the time she reaches puberty her level is down to 300,000. Besides being interesting, what this shows is that a woman "loses" eggs at a considerable rate, so it's not just the five hundred or so eggs she loses when she actually ovulates that depletes her supply, but a natural attrition rate.

That explains why at some point in her life, if she lives long enough, a woman will run out of eggs and her monthly cycles will end. If that were the extent of it, menopause would be no big deal. Most women would welcome menopause, as it would mean the end of having to deal with their periods. But a woman's monthly cycle is regulated by the release of different hormones, and it is the changes in this hormonal activity that cause the difficulties associated with menopause.

In a woman who is having regular monthly cycles, each month, as she's preparing to ovulate (to release an egg), the level of estrogen in her body rises until it peaks just before ovulation occurs. The estrogen tells her body to get ready to receive an egg. Among the commands given is one to the lining of the uterus, the endometrium, to thicken, and it does so by engorging with extra blood. (This is the simplified version, as I said.)

Once she ovulates, the now empty egg sac (the follicle) starts releasing progesterone, which further prepares the woman's body to play host to a fertilized egg. If fertilization doesn't take place, in other words if she doesn't get pregnant, then the levels of both hormones drop dramatically and the uterus sheds its lining, resulting in menstruation (i.e., your period). There are other hormones that trigger other aspects of this process that I'm not going to go into, and females even produce small amounts of testosterone, the male hormone, which aids the libido.

So every month, from the onset of her period as a teenager, called *menarche*, to the time she reaches the menopausal stage, a woman goes through this cycle that is triggered by the release of these various hormones. But while menopause signifies the end of a woman's reproductive life, the rate at which her body releases these hormones can begin to undergo changes years before she actually attains menopause. This stage has been named *perimenopause*, and while the effects are generally not as strong, they can be quite noticeable. During perimenopause, a woman's period sort of goes in stops and starts, and the level of these hormones can get off kilter. Those hormonal imbalances will trigger side effects, like hot flashes. The same is true for menopause, though eventually, as the body gives up the fight of trying to trigger ovulation in a woman who doesn't have any more eggs to give, the imbalance ceases as the hormone levels drop altogether.

Since perimenopause begins before the Whitewater Years, I'm not going to go into this topic in any depth. But if you are experiencing changes but are not yet menopausal, definitely read up on this subject in a book dedicated to this stage in a woman's life and/or ask your doctor about it. Whether or not you decide to take any action, just knowing what is happening to you can be quite a comfort.

Beyond a Cessation of Bleeding

It would be great if that were the end of it, but those hormones that course through a woman's body every month offer her a certain amount of protection for her general well-being. When their levels substantially decrease, women are subject to heart disease, loss of bone density (osteoporosis), mental health problems such as memory loss, and various forms of cancer. Of course throughout much of mankind's existence, fewer women lived long enough to attain menopause. But now that women are living a lot longer, trying to prevent this damage becomes important.

When Does Menopause Set In?

At its most basic, the medical definition says that menopause starts one year after a woman has had her last menstrual period. As she's approaching menopause, her periods will become more irregular. In other words, menopause isn't like a line that a woman crosses, going from having regular periods to having none at all. Instead, she'll start missing periods, even for several months at a time, but then have another one or two at monthly intervals.

Here's an important warning: many women who have been experiencing the signs of approaching menopause, the hot flashes and such, and who don't have a period for a couple of months think that they're now menopausal and can't get pregnant. They engage in unprotected sex and suddenly find themselves, you guessed it, with child. That's the reason doctors say to wait until you have gone an entire year without having any periods before declaring yourself as having reached menopause. That way there won't be any surprise endings to your maternal life.

Why does Mother Nature see to it that a woman loses her capacity to become pregnant? No one knows for sure, though it is thought that it might be dangerous for an older woman to go through the process of labor and giving birth, and so it is a protective mechanism. But since throughout the ages most women never lived long enough to get to the menopausal stage, it seems a little hard to believe that humans would have developed this particular type of protection.

During the initial phase, before the complete cessation of menses has reached that official one-year mark, a woman may experience the short-term symptoms, which can include hot flashes, night sweats, insomnia, a throbbing head, difficulty concentrating, and panic attacks. (She may have also experienced some of these symptoms more mildly during perimenopause, but here I'm speaking of the time period that directly leads to menopause.) Then with actual menopause and the final decrease in hormonal activity comes the risks of the long-term ill effects I mentioned such as osteoporosis and heart disease.

When does all this activity start? The average age of onset of menopause is fifty-one, but it can start as early as forty or not hit until a woman is in her late fifties, though most women arrive at this milestone between forty-five and fifty-five. Now there are some women who naturally become menopausal even younger than forty, while others who have had their ovaries surgically removed or have undergone chemotherapy who will also develop the symptoms of menopause at whichever age they have undergone these medical procedures.

Luckily, the short-term effects of menopause, like the hot flashes, disappear all on their own. How much a woman is affected by these symptoms is relative. All women go through menopause, but in some cultures, the effects seem to be less severe. Is it something in their diet? (For example in Japan, there is a lot of soy in their diet, which contains estrogen-like properties.) Or is it an attitudinal issue? (The Chinese have long treated menopause more lightly.) As I said, I believe enough in the protective possibilities of your attitude to recommend that you do all you can to minimize your reaction to these symptoms.

There are also simple health steps that can be effective. For example, smoking lowers the effect that estrogen has on your body, and women who smoke generally go through menopause two or three years earlier than those who don't. So as the level of your hormones begins to decrease, smoking will cause the changes of menopause to have an even stronger effect. The obvious cure for this is to stop smoking (as if all the other health benefits weren't enough of an incentive). And exercise can help to offset the increased risks that accompany menopause with respect to diseases of the heart, diabetes, and various cancers.

On the other hand, if you're one of those women who have a severe reaction to reaching or approaching menopause, there are alternatives. I can't give you all the details, but I'm going to go over the basics. Your next step should be to ask your doctor about what can be done medically to alleviate your discomfort.

HRT

That there is an avenue of escape is a relatively recent development (since the 1950s), though it makes perfectly good sense; if the problems arise because of a decrease in certain hormones, replacing these hormones artificially will alleviate the situation.

At first women were only given estrogen. Then there was a scare that such treatment increased the risk of endometrial cancer. Then it was discovered that adding progesterone protected women against this cancer. And then . . . well it seems that every day some new study is announced, which only makes it all the more confusing. As an example, I just read a study that says while using HRT may increase the risk of breast cancer, women who take hormones through HRT and who develop breast cancer may survive longer than those who get breast cancer and never took hormonal supplements. So it's one of those "you're damned if you do, damned if you don't" situations.

Here's another one: heart disease is much more dangerous to women than cancer, and HRT offers women significant protection against heart disease. But to obtain this protection, women must be on HRT for a long time, at least ten
years, yet the longer a woman takes HRT, the greater her
risk of getting some form of cancer.

Is There an Answer?

Any woman who is not confused by all of the information
pouring out of the medical community is just not paying attention. And maybe that's a valid approach; ignore all that's
been said and written about HRT and either do what your
grandmother did, which was let nature run its course, or say
to your doctor, "You decide," and wash your hands of the
whole matter. If you're the type who is going to constantly
worry about whether you're making the right decision, then
I suggest you adopt one of these options. Otherwise it will
drive you crazy and the worrying will be much worse than
the actual symptoms of menopause and can even make the
symptoms of menopause worse as well.

While I answer people's questions about sex quite specifi-
cally all day long, I'm sorry to say that when it comes to HRT,
I can't give you one particular answer. Not only is this a very
complicated issue, but there are many individual factors—
like a woman's weight, whether or not she smokes, and
heredity—that must also be taken into consideration when
deciding what is the best course of action. So there is no
doubt that you must consult with your doctor. I would suggest, however, that you buy a book on this subject and study
it carefully before having that conversation. Your doctor is
not going to have the time to give you a complete explanation and so you should at least have the basics down pat.

And if my experience is worth anything, it's going to take you a while to absorb even the basics, unless you already have a degree in biology.

Therefore, I would say that the best approach is to read all you can, consult with your doctor, pick a game plan (HRT or not), and then stop worrying about it for a while. Schedule a check up for six months down the road, and until that time, do your best to forget about menopause and its symptoms.

And though it is your body, as I said earlier, include your partner in this process. If he doesn't want to read an entire book about menopause and HRT, find a magazine article and make him read that. Make sure that he knows enough so that he can act as a sounding board when you have discussions. By sharing the burden of this decision with him it will make it easier on you.

Self-Help

But is there anything you can do besides reading a book and talking to your doctor? Absolutely. One is to make some lifestyle changes, because the better the state of your overall health, the less risks you face. If you're overweight or smoke or have high blood pressure, it is important that you do something about these issues as soon as possible, or you will suffer the consequences over time. To do this will require your spouse's help. It's going to take patience on both your parts, and encouragement, but if you can work together as a team, you can improve your health.

The other important area that I've mentioned is reducing stress. Stress has a significant role to play in combating the effects of menopause. When your body gets stressed out, for whatever reason, your adrenal glands produce hormones related to the "fight or flight" reflex. To make these hormones, it steals the production material needed to make other hormones, including those for estrogen and progesterone. Now if a woman is already having problems with balancing her hormones because of perimenopause or menopause, stress exacerbates this imbalance even more, and she is going to feel the symptoms more strongly than ever. So whatever your doctor and you decide to do about HRT, you can definitely improve your reaction to these changes in your life by reducing the amount of stress you have to face. And as I said before, the one person who can be most helpful in this is your husband or significant other.

Case History: Carole and Ed

Ed knew that there was this period that women went through called menopause, but what this meant exactly was somewhat sketchy, until his wife, Carole, began exhibiting the signs of menopause. Ed had always prided himself on being able to read his wife, but now her mood swings were such that he was feeling punch drunk. At first, he would get angry when she acted in ways that to him were irrational, but then he decided to read up on menopause. Carole had several books on the subject, and one night, Ed stayed up until 2 in the morning going through them. The most important thing he read, from his point of view, was that the symptoms of menopause would eventually settle down so that her mood swings were only temporary. Once he understood that, he was better able to handle her menopause. Instead of reacting angrily when she appeared to be irrational, he would take a deep breath and either say something consoling or just walk away. His change in attitude had quite a positive effect on both of them, and it wasn't long before he got his "old" wife back.

What a Partner Can Do

In cases when a woman cannot achieve orgasm, I tell her to masturbate and, when she's figured out exactly what motions and caresses work for her, to then show her partner what he must do. In other words, rather than blame her partner for not being able to bring her to orgasm, she has to figure out what she needs and then teach him, as he can't be expected to guess.

When it comes to relieving stress, the exact same rule applies. There are literally hundreds of sources of stress, but each one of these impacts an individual differently. For example, some people are driven crazy by being stuck in traffic, while others take a more fatalistic approach and pay it no mind. If you have two people in a car in a traffic jam and they each have a different reaction, you can imagine that there is going to be some miscommunication that is going to add to the overall level of stress. In this type of situation, it's better to sympathize with the frustrated person, which will help to diffuse their emotions, at least to some degree.

But now picture the opposite scenario. The person who doesn't care about the traffic jam criticizes the other for being so impatient. One likely outcome is that the impatient person is going to redirect any negative feelings from the traffic jam toward his or her partner's criticism. The other person is then going to answer back, and even if traffic does start moving again, the couple will be at each other's throats and the level of tension will soar.

Admittedly it's impossible to live with another human being without some chafing going on. You're not Siamese twins and you're going to react differently to various stimuli, and that's going to cause some friction. But normally each person shows some restraint and these little spats don't get out of hand. But when a woman is feeling the effects of menopause, her reaction may not be entirely under her control. With her hormones in an unbalanced state, she may overreact to something that she wouldn't have before. And so a little spat can grow into a major conflict, and her stress level will go even higher, making her symptoms that much worse. The solution is for her partner to act as a shock absorber. He has to understand what is going on, and, rather than take up the gauntlet she may have laid down, step around it and try to diffuse the tension. He has to do this because he loves her and because he understands that for a certain amount of time, she needs him to give her some added support as she goes through these changes.

The only way that he is going to agree to this role change is if he understands what is happening to his wife and accepts that for a time she needs his help to overcome the difficulties she is having. If they talk about all of this and come to some sort of agreement, then by working together they should be able to minimize the stress she is under, and that in turn will help to diminish the strength of the symptoms of menopause. But as with the example I gave about orgasms, she is going to have to tell him what raises her stress level the most. She has to say, "Honey, please let's not talk about that" or "Please don't do that any more, it's driving me crazy," and he'll have to agree to listen. She can't use menopause as an excuse to try to completely change his behavior, as that will never work. But she does have to let him know what things irritate her the most, and he has to agree to make some adjustments so as to minimize her levels of stress.

What Else He Can Do

There are other ways that a man can help his partner besides absorbing some extra shocks instead of reacting to them. Exercise is very helpful, both for improving health and for reducing levels of stress. He should encourage his wife to get as much exercise as possible. And exercise is even more fun if you have a partner, so besides offering her a membership at a gym, he should make time to exercise with her, for example, asking her to go for a walk or to play some tennis or whatever. And sharing these activities will also be helpful in strengthening their relationship, as these will also be times when conversation will be possible.

One of the side effects of menopause is that women more easily put on weight. Fat cells produce estrogen and so one of the body's defenses with regards to making up for the loss of estrogen from the ovaries is to add fat cells that will manufacture estrogen. In order for her not to put on a lot more weight, she's going to have to carefully watch her diet as well as get exercise. If he insists she prepare meals with as much caloric content as she did before, that is going to make it more difficult for her to maintain her weight. If he doesn't want to cut down on his intake of food, one thing he could do, for example, is have a slightly larger lunch so that he could accept having a slightly leaner dinner.

And if she does put on some weight, he should not be critical of her body. That will only make her feel more stressful, which will lower her level of estrogen production and cause her to gain even more weight. While he doesn't have to give compliments that he doesn't feel, he may, for example, enjoy the fact that her breasts may have grown, as they are comprised mostly of fat tissue, and can definitely let her know that he finds a positive change in that particular increase. He can also try his best to compliment her on other features such as her face or hair or whatever other aspects of her that he may find worthy of praise.

I know that there are men who purposefully won't compliment a wife who has put on weight fearing that she'll feel

37

that all is well with the way she looks and put aside any effort of losing the weight. That, in fact, may be how a man would react; but not a woman. She knows that she has some pounds to lose and will not lose sight of that no matter how many compliments her husband gives her. But if she doesn't get any compliments, she will then get depressed about her looks, and that will add to her level of stress and cause her to gain even more weight. So men should keep the compliments coming, no matter whether he likes the changes that accompany menopause or not.

One more thing he can do is to change his overall attitude toward her monthly cycle. Most men want as little to do with a woman's period as possible, and who can blame them? If women weren't forced to deal with this regular bleeding, they'd avoid it too. But if his overall attitude is going to change as a woman approaches menopause, then it's going to have to be a subject that is on the table. But let me say again, he will get something in return for being an active partner. By asking questions and talking about menopause, the couple will grow closer and their level of intimacy will increase. That is bound to have a positive effect on their sex life.

Of course some couples have always been very intimate with each other, and the men in those couples will already be in tune with menopausal changes and will naturally be an active partner in helping the women to deal with them. But in couples where women's problems were just that, such a separation also affects their overall level of intimacy. By becoming partners in her menopausal changes, they can undoubtedly become closer and improve their relationship.

CHAPTER 3

Other Female Health Problems

A S A WOMAN ENTERS HER WHITEWATER YEARS, in addition to the medical problems related to menopause, she will be faced with other health issues as well. Some will be purely cosmetic, such as graying hair, wrinkles, and liver spots. Others will be signs of aging that, while annoying, are unavoidable, such as the need for reading glasses or a hearing aid. And then there are the more serious medical conditions, such as heart disease, diabetes, cancer, and so forth.

I couldn't possibly give you advice on all the health-related issues that a woman can encounter as she grows older, in part because I am not a physician, as I said, but also because of space limitations. My area of expertise, as you know, is sex and relationships and so I'm going to do some picking and choosing among this medical cabinet full of problems and offer advice on how these problems may affect your love and sex life and what you can do about it.

General Advice

Let me start with some general advice that applies to most of these medical conditions. It's sad, at least from my point of view, that many doctors are just as reluctant to talk about sexual functioning as their patients are to bring it up. They're not given adequate training in how to hold such conversations, and while they may mention a sexual issue, if the patient is the least bit reticent, they'll breathe a sigh of relief and push on to something else. But most patients brought up in this society, which still retains much of the Puritan ethic, don't communicate easily about their sex lives, even when it comes to asking their physician questions, and so in many cases the only way for doctors to find out about this aspect of their patients' lives is to do some probing. This isn't prying to be nosy or voyeuristic; it's asking questions in order to get the patient to reveal a physical aspect of her life that otherwise would remain hidden. As a consequence of all this shyness, on the part of both doctors and their patients, many people's sex lives are negatively impacted in ways that they shouldn't be.

Sex after a Heart Attack

Case History: Richard and Sarah

Richard was fifty-five when he had his heart attack. Before it happened, he thought he was in good physical shape, though his cholesterol had been a bit elevated. His recovery went well, and when he got home he duly followed his doctor's orders and changed his diet and made other lifestyle changes to protect himself from having another attack. Though his doctor had said that he could resume having sex, when he first returned home from the hospital he was in no mood for it. But after about a month had passed and the memory of what happened started to fade, his libido kicked in. When he approached his wife, Sarah, and started cuddling with her in a way that before would have let her know that he was interested in having sex, she pulled away. He asked her what was wrong, and she admitted that she was terrified that if they had sex, he might have another heart attack.

The case of Richard and Sarah is fairly commonplace in such situations. The fear of causing another heart attack could remove all desire for sex for the victim, the spouse, or both. This fear is natural, but it must be overcome. The worst scenario occurs when instead of discussing what is going through their minds, they just sidestep the issue of resuming sex. If this goes on for too long, sex can become permanently removed from the table, and theirs becomes a sexless relationship.

While in some rare cases sex is not possible because one partner has such a bad heart, in general sex is not so taxing that it needs to be ruled out. Some doctors will give their patients specific instructions, but many do not. And if patients won't ask questions, then their sex lives will needlessly go down the drain.

While people can live without sex, it is part of the glue that holds a relationship together. It is also a part of good health. If both husband and wife are sexually frustrated, their nerves may become more easily frayed and the resulting stress will take a toll on both of them. So patients and doctors should do all they can to prevent sexless marriages from arising needlessly.

When you're checking out a doctor, your main concern, of course, is to make sure he or she knows about their specialty, so that if it's a cardiologist you are seeking, you want the best cardiologist, not the one who is most likely to talk about sex after surgery. But you also don't want to give up your sex life without a fight either. So in such cases, you—meaning both husband and wife—are going to have to take the bull by the horns and ask the proper questions. In the case of heart disease, you want to have spelled out for you what is appropriate and what is not. For example, there may be some positions that would be too taxing while others might pose less risk. This is a topic that you shouldn't have to guess about because if that's what you're doing, there's going to be a nagging doubt in the back of your mind and that's going to spoil much if not all of your pleasure, perhaps enough to prevent one or both parties from having an orgasm. That in turn could spark resentment, which leads to added tension, which would be bad for each partner's health, including the damaged heart. So this isn't idle chatter. Getting sexual satisfaction is important, and it is not a subject that should be pushed under the rug. You must ask the heart specialist detailed questions so that you have an exact road map of what is safe and what might not be.

If necessary, you could use a sex therapist as a go-between. A sex therapist is not a medical doctor, so the therapist can never tell you whether having sex is safe or not. But it might be easier for your doctor to talk with the therapist, who could then relay the information to you. Hopefully you won't need this type of intervention, but if you find yourself in a situation where you feel you're not getting answers to your questions, you should think of using a go-between.

Other Medical Conditions

Any couple that is dealing with a heart condition of either or both partners doesn't need me to tell them that this is a problem area when it comes to sex. But there are many other conditions where the potential impact on your sex life may not be as apparent. I'm going to highlight some of those here that particularly affect women. Men get their own chapter a bit later on.

An Overactive Bladder

Many women develop what is labeled an overactive bladder. (This condition may also be called a hyperactive or irritable bladder, as well as urge incontinence.) Some women have this at an early age, but many more develop it in their Whitewater Years or beyond, that is to say after menopause. The estimates range as high as seventeen million Americans suffer from this condition with almost 50 percent of women over sixty-five reporting some problems in this area. For women who have an overactive bladder, it means that they will be visiting their nearest toilet every couple of hours. When this becomes serious enough, women with this condition are afraid to leave the house, so that their social lives are ruined. In its most extreme form, it ends up turning into incontinence, meaning that the woman cannot always get to the toilet in time. One way of measuring how widespread incontinence is in this country is to note that more money is spent on adult diapers than on those for children. And whether or not people can tell, women who wear these garments believe others can tell, by smell perhaps, and so many refuse to leave their homes, ruining their social life and ending any possibility of working.

Among the "victims" of an overactive bladder is often the woman's sex life. Even if she doesn't actually leak urine when engaging in sex, the fear that she might leak or else suddenly have the urge to "go" will have a serious impact on her libido. So rather than risk having to jump out of bed to run to the bathroom, or risk even further embarrassment, many women with an overactive bladder give up having sex.

And you know what the worst part of all of this is? Very often it is unnecessary. Treatment is available, but many people are too ashamed to ask their doctors about it.

The Shame Factor

This is a phenomenon I know quite well. Many, many people suffer from some sort of sexual dysfunction that is definitely treatable, but they never seek out a sex therapist for help. The reason is they are ashamed to admit it. While urinary function is no different from any other type of functioning, because the genitals are involved, our Puritan ethic raises its head and these sorts of ailments are lumped in with sexual problems and kept hidden by far too many people of both sexes. So women who wouldn't hesitate to get eyeglasses to fix a problem with their vision or go to a lung specialist to alleviate their asthma won't speak to their doctors about issues having to do with urination. And I'm not just talking about sex here, but about their constant need to go to the toilet, too.

This is a sad state of affairs. We've gone through the so-called sexual revolution and you can't pick up a woman's magazine without seeing the word *sex* on the cover, and yet when it comes to people's personal lives, the deep inhibitions passed on from previous generations still have a very strong effect.

Since I'm not a physician, I'm not going to get very deep into bladder problems here, but since I mentioned this condition was treatable, I do owe you some sort of explanation. Doctors don't always know why people develop an overactive bladder. For some it's the result of a stroke. In others, the cause is diabetes. People with high blood pressure have a 40 percent increased risk of suffering from a leaking bladder.

Women who have had children share a greater risk. And obese people are also more likely candidates. While this condition affects older women in greater numbers, it has been estimated that as many as 25 percent of women under sixty-five also suffer from an overactive bladder, if not on a daily basis, then from time to time.

Again, while the exact cause is unknown, there are two suspected sources of the problem, both having to do with the nervous system. In the first, the muscles surrounding the bladder start to contract without the person being in control so that the urge to urinate cannot be suppressed. In the other, there is some sort of short circuit between the brain and these muscles, resulting in a lack of control.

But a woman doesn't have to understand what is causing her all this discomfort. All she needs to know is that there is medication, such as DITROPAN XL® (oxybutynin chloride) extended release tablets,[1] that may help provide the needed control, and so by talking to her doctor about it and being given a prescription, she may feel the sudden urge to urinate much less frequently. This type of oral medication is approved for the treatment of overactive bladder and is well tolerated by and quite effective for most women. For women who suffer from an overactive bladder, it can potentially change their lives.

If a woman assumes that the problem is caused by her aging body and that there is no hope of regaining the control she once had, and if she's feeling a great deal of embarrassment over what is happening, then she's not as likely to ask her doctor about it. That's why we must get the word out to people suffering from an overactive bladder that there is something that can be done and urge them to make an appointment with a physician as soon as possible. Your doctor wants to help you, but he or she can't guess that you are having difficulties. You have to make the appointment and describe symptoms of all types that you are having.

What is particularly sad is when a person goes to her doctor for a checkup, is asked if she has any problems to report, and she can't gather up the courage to mention this particular one, or any having to do with her genitals. This is very similar to the adage about bravery that says the brave man dies only once while the coward dies a thousand deaths. The woman who cannot find the will to tell her doctor about a problem such as this may avoid the embarrassment at that particular moment, but she then suffers throughout the rest of her life from always having to run to the bathroom.

Interstitial Cystitis

With an overactive bladder, embarrassment at potential leakage is the reason that people stay home, stop socializing, and stop having sex with their partner. With a heart condition the problem is fear. But with this next condition, interstitial cystitis (IC), the main reason a woman will stop having sex with her husband, as well as having many other problems to cope with, is pain.

Case History: Terry-Jo

Terry-Jo first noticed the symptoms of IC when she was twenty-one years old. The pain would wake her up all through the night, and she was constantly exhausted. She had become a professional golfer, but often times she had to drop out of tournaments because of the frequent urge to urinate. She wouldn't admit what the real reason was and would make up other physical injuries. IC was literally ruining her entire life.

Interstitial cystitis is thought to originate by a breakdown of the lining of the bladder. This allows a leakage of irritants, which causes chronic inflammation and pain. One result is a constant need to urinate, as with an overactive bladder, but potentially with even much more frequency, for example, as many as twenty-five times a night (though IC is sometimes labeled "overactive bladder, dry," as there is no actual incontinence). But IC can be much worse than an overactive bladder because of the potential accompanying pain, which can be considerable and is almost always in evidence during sexual intercourse. This pain may not be felt in the early stages of the disease, but as it gradually progresses over time, it can make IC quite debilitating. Women with this disease have had to give up employment, drop out of school, or suffer many other ill effects.

Easily Misdiagnosed

Because of the pain, IC is often misdiagnosed as a urinary tract infection (UTI) or a symptom of a sexually transmitted disease (STD), both of which can have many of the same symptoms. But the standard treatments for a UTI or an STD will be completely ineffective if the true cause is IC. What is needed is a medication to repair the lining of the bladder. Up until recently, there was a limited awareness of an oral medication available in the United States that can provide relief for some women who have IC.

ELMIRON® (pentosan polysulfate sodium) capsules[2] is an oral medication that is FDA approved to treat the symptoms of IC. It has been suggested that it reinforces the protective layer of the bladder's lining. By treating the underlying problem, it may act as a buffer, preventing the irritants in the urine from reaching the cells that cause the painful reaction. It's taken as a capsule, and after a woman has taken it for the prescribed period, the buildup of the bladder's protective layer can lessen the effects of IC dramatically. This drug is well tolerated by women, with fewer than 5 percent showing adverse symptoms.

But to fulfill that hope, IC must first be correctly diagnosed. Because the symptoms of IC are similar to those of other conditions, it takes some persistence on the part of the doctor and patient to get to the bottom of things. In most instances, a doctor will assume it's a UTI, as they are quite common, and prescribe the necessary drugs for that particular disease. If the patient doesn't return to the doctor to let him or her know that the problem is persisting, the additional tests for IC will never be performed, and the symptoms of IC will only get worse.

Another problem in diagnosing IC is that the resulting pain may be felt in other parts of the body. The nerves of the bladder merge with the nerves of the colon, rectum, and uterus in the spinal cord. As a result, a patient with an irritated bladder may perceive pain in any one or a combination of areas including the pelvic region, the inside of the thighs, the labia, deep inside the vagina, the urethra, the vulva, and the perineum. Obviously this makes it much more difficult for a doctor to pinpoint the origin of the woman's pain.

IC at Any Age

IC can strike women of any age, but a large problem occurs when it hits older women because they may, as with an overactive bladder, wrongly assume that the problem is associated with menopause or simple aging. They may have seen their mothers or grandmothers develop a greater urge to urinate and so assume that the same thing is happening to them. Since the pain, which normally will drive her to a doctor, may take years to become severe, a woman may suffer all that time because she assumed that there was nothing to be done.

With sex, pain that is felt in the vulva, for example, particularly after intercourse, may not be easily identified as a problem in the bladder. In fact, it's quite likely that a woman with IC will go to the wrong doctor! If a woman is feeling pain in her vagina, especially after intercourse, she's likely to visit her gynecologist. But it is a urologist who would be most likely to spot a case of IC. So if you were to go to a gynecologist with vaginal pain and this doctor was not succeeding in coming up with the answer, then you need to exhibit the patience to keep going back until your doctor decides that it may not be something that he or she is familiar with and sends you to see a urologist.

Because IC is complicated to find, it is somewhat understandable that a woman who has gone to the doctor and not met with success with treating her pain may just decide to give up and abandon the joys that come from having sex. As I've already said, sexual frustration can lead to all sorts of problems, including an end to a marriage, so any pain that leads to a cessation of sexual activity must be looked into until the cause is found. And as with an overactive bladder, stress can make the symptoms worse, if for no other reason than that stress reduces a person's pain threshold and so it can make the pain of IC seem even worse than it is. Therefore anything you can do to reduce stress is important in the fight against IC, and something that increases stress, like not having sex, can make it worse.

When it comes to your health, what you must not do is stay on the raft letting yourself get thrown from side to side. If routine treatment does not leave you satisfied, you have to climb into your kayak and start paddling, going against the current if need be. This isn't always easy. If you've always kept your sex life under wraps, it's not easy to tell your doctor that you and your husband are not having sex because it has become painful for you, but that is what must be done. And if you've gone back to your doctor several times and he seems ready to give up the fight, then it's your job to urge him on.

Don't Play Doctor

Some women who suffer from IC decide that they can treat the pain that accompanies it themselves. For example, they'll urinate before engaging in sex in the hopes of alleviating the pain by emptying their bladder. Or they'll avoid prolonged intercourse. Or they'll try positions that minimize contact to the bladder. Or they'll take over-the-counter pain killers. In the end, none of these "treatments" is going to effectively end the pain of IC, and so what many women do is put an end to their sex life. That's not going to help either, though it will alleviate the specific pain that comes from having sex; but the better course, by far, is to see a doctor and explain what has been happening.

How Your Spouse Might React

Now I realize that it may not be easy to tell your husband what is going on. The simpler way around this pain might be to avoid sex. You can go to bed earlier than he does and then feign that you are asleep. Or you can find work to do so that eventually he gives up and goes to sleep first. Is embarrassment the only reason that you would act this way? Not necessarily. Perhaps your husband has been making fun of you for having to go to the bathroom so much. That could make you angry at him for not understanding, which in turn would make you even less interested in wanting to restore your sex life back to its original, healthy condition. Or you might be afraid that he's going to push you to go to the doctor, and you're too ashamed to talk about it with your physician. Or you might be under the misconception that there is no cure and that sex is over between the two of you and you don't want to be the one to break this awful news to him.

I can't repeat myself too often when I say that the best thing is for the two of you, meaning you and your husband, to act as a team in such matters. Don't hide what is really going on. He may end up doing some nagging, but maybe that's just what you need to get the condition cared for. And if it does mean admitting that sex may be out of the question until you get to the bottom of what is happening, at least that gives the two of you some hope. But avoiding sex only means that your partner is likely to think something else is going on, that you're no longer attracted to him, and that can cause a permanent cessation to sex.

Pain and Sex

While IC causes painful intercourse, which is an obvious obstacle to having a good sexual relationship, any type of pain can cause serious problems to a couple's sex life. One common source of pain that may first appear in the Whitewater Years is arthritis. Not only does pain, in general, make it more difficult to become aroused, but when the pain is associated with a particular joint, it can make the movements required for intercourse uncomfortable and perhaps even impossible.

Most people in their fifties who suffer from arthritis have milder symptoms, which may be treatable with simple pain relief medicine, perhaps even the over-the-counter variety. But since there is no "cure" for arthritis, there's always the possibility that a mild case will get progressively worse, and so it's important that you begin to manage how you will cope with arthritis from its very earliest stages. What this requires, as with many of the other conditions we've discussed, is a higher level of intimacy. The positions that you've become accustomed to may no longer be appropriate. For example, arthritis in the hands or arms could make it uncomfortable for the man to hold himself up in the missionary position, which is by far the most popular in our culture. Such an occurrence should not spell the end of a couple's love life. In fact, experimenting on new positions could add some spice to their sex life. But that is only going to work if they are truly intimate and can have fun trying out new positions. If one doesn't work out, they have to be able to laugh about it—not withdraw from each other—and try another one. The more experimentation they do, the better.

To some couples this may seem obvious. But there are a great many couples in this country who, despite having sex, are very reserved about their sexual habits. A routine develops and they stick to it. They might both have great orgasms from it and see no need to add some variety. But then when a situation like this comes along, they have a difficult time dealing with it. Knowing that there will be some "complications" in your sex life as you get older should be the stimulus you need to start making some changes as soon as possible. It's much better if you can at least begin to add some twists to your lovemaking when you're healthy and can still fall back on the tried and true for sexual fulfillment than to wait until the old ways are no longer an option and you're more likely to give up when confronted with failure trying new ones.

Challenges to a Woman's Appearance

I take all statistics with a grain of salt, but whatever the statistics may say, it does seem that many more women are being diagnosed with breast cancer these days than ever before. And that, in turn, means that many more women are having to deal with having one or both breasts removed. While a woman may be able to hide the fact that she has lost a breast from the general public by wearing a prosthesis, the one person to whom she thinks this loss matters most, her husband, is the one person she really can't hide it from.

Many women opt for breast reconstruction surgery at the same time their breast is removed, while others feel no such need. Here's my opinion on the matter. Have you ever seen a photograph of a woman with a breast removed? I think you'll agree that it's somewhat shocking. And that's looking at a stranger. Imagine what a husband is going to feel seeing his wife with a scar where one of her breasts once was. Admittedly it is a sight that one can get used to, but there's no guarantee that every man will be able to get used to it. So rather than be stoic, assuming that cost is not a factor, I would tell women to go ahead with reconstruction.

There's another reason I feel this way. There are no guarantees in life. You may have a husband today, but either death or divorce could strike and then you'd be searching for a new partner. Your husband swore to love you no matter what, but no other man has made the same vow. I'm not saying it's impossible to find a man who won't be willing to overlook a missing breast, but it does make it that much more difficult. And while a reconstructed breast doesn't look exactly like a real one, it's close enough that it makes the hurdle that much lower.

With or without reconstructive surgery, there is going to be a psychological blow to both partners following a mastectomy. The woman may lose confidence in her appearance to the point of lowering her libido. The man may fear his reaction, and that fear alone could put a damper on his sex drive. Here is a situation where counseling could provide much relief. It might be suggested by a counselor that you speak with other couples who have gone through this, and the counselor could refer you to the proper groups. Just hearing their stories may set you at ease. But even having a counselor reassure you that you can be your old selves again will be very helpful. In cases such as this it is easy to work yourselves up to such a degree that it is impossible for you to get beyond the problem. This will depend on an individual's personality, but you can't always tell in advance when a particular trauma will cause more damage than was expected. So if you feel that the loss of a breast, or any such change, is not something that the two of you can handle alone, go for help.

Now the removal of a breast is one of the most traumatic of the possible appearance changes that a woman may go through as she gets older. As I've already mentioned, with menopause can come an increase in weight, and then there is the graying of her hair, added wrinkles, drier skin, possibly increased hirsuteness, and so forth. Some women spend fortunes on plastic surgery and the like to try to fight those changes, but not only is that expensive, it's not always effective in the long term as plastic surgery doesn't last forever and, after a series of repairs, can leave the person looking worse than if they'd never started the process to begin with.

While such attempts at keeping Father Time at bay may be more necessary for single women who are trying to attract a new man, for women in long-term relationships, I think it is better to compensate for these changes rather than try to fight them. There is no doubt that men are attracted to physical beauty, but as a man ages, so does his overall level of arousal. Where he might have obtained an erection just from the sight of a long slender leg at one time, he's going to need more than that once he hits a certain age. And that's where the wife can have an advantage. If she's learned what pleases him and maintained an intimate relationship with him, even if his eyes stray from time to time, the rest of him is less likely to follow his gaze. On the other hand, if she spends too much time worrying about her looks but doesn't take care of their relationship, then she's much more likely to lose that battle.

I'm not saying that a woman can just let herself go; far from it. You do have to maintain your appearance, if not for your partner's sake, then for your own self-esteem. But while you can try to look your best for your age range, if you try too hard to make it seem that you are a generation younger than you actually are, the odds are that you are going to fail. Such a failure will make you feel even worse. So do your best to accept these changes while also doing your best to make the most of what you have.

The Intimacy Factor, Again

Looks are only one arrow in your quiver when it comes to keeping your partner interested in you sexually. If that arrow isn't as sharp as it once was, then you're probably going to have to use some of the other ones. I'm going to get into this in more detail in another chapter, but it's something that had to be mentioned here. And the most important one, the one I've mentioned over and over again, is to build up the intimacy between you and your mate.

The Whitewater Years present a fork in the road. Down one path lies a pulling apart and a decrease, possibly even a cessation, of your love life. Down the other path lies a change in the way you have sex, but an accompanied increase in intimacy and a closeness and warmth that can actually make your sex life better. Where before the Whitewater Years you could sort of hold the middle ground, that's an option that is going to be much more difficult. Changes are going to occur in each of you and you're going to have to adapt to those changes.

I'm sorry that I have to keep harping on this message, but I know that it's the biggest stumbling block that couples encounter at this stage of their lives. It's easy to say you're going to make those alterations, but it's easier to let them slip by. So not only have I said this before, but rest assured that I will say it again, and again.

The Medicine Cabinet

As we get older and develop even mild health problems, the probability grows that the stack of pills that you end up swallowing each morning is going to grow. While the drug companies do test their products, it is well known that each individual will react to a particular drug in a different way. So while one drug used to bring down high blood pressure may not cause a side effect in one person, that same drug might make another person lose all his or her desire for sex, or increase desire.

Whatever side effects you feel, whether it has to do with sex or not, do not assume that there isn't anything that can be done about it. First of all, a slight change in the dosage could alleviate the side effect without reducing the effectiveness of the drug. Or there may be another drug on the market that is equally effective for the problem it is supposed to manage, such a high blood pressure, but won't give you the side effect that the other drug did. Our bodies are all sufficiently different that it is impossible to say for sure how a particular medicine will affect any one individual. Now your doctor is going to make certain that the medicine prescribed acts positively on the condition he or she is trying to fix, so the doctor will check to see whether the blood pressure medicine was bringing down your blood pressure. But unless you tell the doctor that you believe that this very same medicine has removed your desire for sex, he or she is not going to know that. But if you speak up, the doctor can give you another medication that hopefully will control your blood pressure but won't also destroy your sex life.

There's another side to this. There are some people who, when they find that a particular medicine is ruining their sex lives, or making them miserable for some other reason, just stop taking the medication. Obviously that is contraindicated. It is much better to talk to your doctor about your sex life than to skip your medication and risk some serious complication.

And what if all the medications for high blood pressure lower your libido? Perhaps that will give you the added incentive to exercise more and change your diet and do whatever else you can so as not to have to take this medication, or at least take it in a lower dosage. Your doctor may also allow you to go off the medicine for a time, being careful to monitor your blood pressure during this time period. (If you purchase a device that measures blood pressure at home, that may make it easier for your doctor to give his permission for this.) That way you can engage in the pleasures of sex and look forward to the next period when that can take place, while you undergo a period of taking the medication in your regular dose.

Depression

While depression affects both men and women, there are more older women who are affected by this than men. One reason is that there are more older women than men, in terms of pure numbers, but that's not the only reason. One has to do with hormonal changes. Both sexes have a reduced amount of sex hormones, but because of menopause, women suffer this loss to a greater degree than do men and it occurs over a shorter period of time. This can play a role in depression. Another possible cause has to do with appearance. Since women lean more heavily on their appearance to attract attention of the opposite sex than do men, the loss of their looks can have a stronger negative effect on their psyche. And since women are more likely to give in to their emotions, if they start a downward slide in spirits, it can carry them much further than it might a man.

Depressed or Just Cranky

When a young person starts acting depressed, there's a good chance that friends and relatives will notice and try to get the person to take some action. When someone who is a little older shows signs of depression, there is a tendency to think that all people of a certain age start to get cranky or grumpy and that it's just a sign of the passing years rather than something treatable. Of course this image of grumpiness is just a form of discrimination. And it is certainly not justified when it comes to someone in his or her Whitewater Years, who is anything but "old."

There are many signs of depression, including changes in sleep patterns, eating problems, excessive crying, but the one that most concerns me is the loss of libido. It should be obvious that someone who is depressed and has lost her interest in life would also lose her interest in sex. On the other hand, because sex is something done with a partner, it can also be one of the first noticeable signs of depression, assuming it's recognized as being a sign of depression. That's why it's important for spouses to talk about their sex life and not just bury their heads in the sand and pretend that nothing has changed.

The communications about sex should not be allowed to turn into a fight. This is not about who is doing what to whom, but trying to get to the bottom of any loss of libido. As you have seen, it could be pain, or medication, or depression, and it may not be immediately apparent, even to the person who has suffered the loss, what the cause actually is.

Now I've said that two heads are better than one, and that's true. But they have to be working toward the same goal. Otherwise, if they're butting heads, then no progress is going to be made. In fact, if one party is depressed, he or she probably won't have the energy to fight and the condition will only worsen.

What to Do

Some types of depression are subject to therapy while others require medication. But no matter the severity, it is better to begin treatment as soon as possible. The longer a person remains depressed, the deeper the depression will become, and the harder it will be for him or her to come out of it. So if one spouse notices that his or her partner is acting depressed, it's important not to shrug it off, but to get the help that partner needs.

A depressed person may not have the inner strength to seek help. If your spouse were to break his or her leg, it would be obvious that you would have to help him or her to get to the doctor's office. Your spouse would be in severe pain and in no shape to drive or maybe even to call a doctor. But sometimes that person with a broken leg might be more capable of getting help than someone who is depressed. If that person can reach a phone, he or she can dial 911 and get assistance. And since that person can immediately recognize that he or she has an injury, there is a high motivation to reach for that phone. But a depressed person might not recognize that he or she could get treatment. And that person's very problem, depression, will make it all the more difficult to pick up a phone and ask for help. So it's very important that their partner take an active role.

Protecting Yourself against Depression

To some extent, you can protect yourself against depression. If you know that you will soon be facing some change that may make you depressed, and especially if you've had to be treated for depression at some other point in your life, then it would be wise to make preparations. For example, in the period right after your last child goes off to college, try not to sit around the empty house moping. Make plans ahead of time to have dinner with friends, see a show, take a class, book time at your local tennis courts, and so forth. The more active you are, the harder it will be to become depressed. So find ways to inoculate yourself against depression, even if that means going to a therapist ahead of time so that you're properly prepared or, if appropriate, medicated.

Case History: Rose and Frank

After spending more than twenty years going on vacations with their children, Rose and Frank finally took a vacation by themselves. They spent four days in a bed-and-breakfast with a romantic four-poster bed and a hot tub in the room. Their sex life had dwindled over the years, down to once a week, but during their four-day getaway, they made love once or twice a day. Rose had arthritis in her hips that had made certain positions difficult, but she discovered that after sitting in the hot tub for a while, the pain was greatly relieved.

OTHER FEMALE HEALTH PROBLEMS

This mini-vacation made them realize that their sex life wasn't necessarily stuck in low gear but could be raised back up if they put their minds to it. When they got back home, they made a point of doing more romantic things together, had a hot tub installed in their basement, and while they didn't make love every day, they did find themselves having sex two or three times as often as before.

It's Not All Bad

Now I've mentioned all sorts of ailments that might begin to affect you in your Whitewater Years, starting with menopause and ending with depression, at least ending at this point. But the last thing I want to do is to depress you about this new stage in your life. Yes, you have to take certain precautions, but that doesn't mean your life is over.

I've always enjoyed skiing, but I've actually done more skiing, and become a better skier, since I entered my Whitewater Years. And at age seventy-four, I still go skiing. The reason? I had more time and income and so could travel to resorts where the ski conditions were better. Now it's true I take fewer risks than when I was younger, but I have even more fun because I'm in better control. So don't go around thinking that your life has peaked because you've entered your Whitewater Years. In some areas, yes it may have peaked, but not in others. You may no longer be able to be the best singles player at your tennis club, but you could still be part of the best doubles team. You might not be able to have as many drinks as you used to without suffering terribly the next morning, but you can now afford to sip the finest of wines in moderate portions. In other words, there are silver linings to these clouds, and it's important that you seek them out.

Notes

1. DITROPAN XL is a trademark of Ortho-McNeil Pharmaceutical, Inc.

2. ELMIRON is a registered trademark of IVAX Research, Inc., under license to Ortho-McNeil Pharmaceutical, Inc.

CHAPTER **4**

When Man's Best Friend
Lets Him Down

L ITTLE BOYS DON'T THINK VERY MUCH ABOUT
their penises. Some boys realize that it feels
good to touch it, but for the most part, it's
not the most important part of their anatomy. But then, as
they reach puberty, they develop a much deeper interest in
that organ. It's no longer a mild pleasure that they receive
from their penises but a very dramatic one; one that many
young men find too good to pass up, even if they have to
cause those sensations themselves.

The Refractory Period

After several decades of learning to adapt to one another, the
Whitewater Years will bring some changes to the relationship between a man and his penis. But before I get into these,
I need to introduce a few concepts that I'll be using to describe what is going to take place.

The first one is called the *refractory period*. The refractory period is the time it takes a man to have a new erection
after he's had an orgasm. In some young men there is basically no refractory period. They can have an orgasm without

losing their erection and start having intercourse again immediately. However, most young men do lose their erection once they've ejaculated, and the length of time it takes before their penises can become erect once again (i.e., how long the refractory period lasts) will depend on several factors, including their natural ability and how much stimulation they are getting. If a man's partner puts her mouth on his penis and starts sucking, then the amount of time it will take for him to get another erection will be a lot shorter than if he puts his clothes back on and heads out the door. But some young men won't be able to have a new erection right away no matter how much effort his partner puts into helping him. So right from the start, you have to understand that the refractory period for men is variable.

But no matter at which point on the refractory period scale a man is to begin with, as he gets older, the refractory period will lengthen. Just as there was a variation in the original ability to get a new erection, there will be quite a variation on how much longer it takes as the years pass. But no matter how short that period was originally, the refractory period is going to get longer as the years stretch out.

Psychogenic Erection

Next on my list of terms is *psychogenic erection*. When a young man sees something sexy, he can voluntarily get an erection without doing anything. (Sometimes young men get erections for absolutely no reason at all, as do many men when they first wake up in the morning, but I'm not interested in those phenomena at present.) Every man will have a slightly different definition of what is sexy, and in the case of gay men, it will be much different from that of a heterosexual male. But while the cause may differ, the effect will be the same. For one man, the anticipation that comes from seeing the opening credits of a porno video will be enough to make his penis become hard, while another man will need the sight of the first naked body, and a third may actually need to see two people having sex to become erect. But in all three cases, the man's penis will become erect without any physical stimulation. That type of erection is called a psychogenic erection.

Just as the refractory period changes with the passing of years, so too does a man's ability to have a psychogenic erection. At first it will take more and more visual or mental stimulation for him to become erect. Then it may be an off and on again sort of situation, so that at times some sort of sexual stimulus will cause an erection and at other times it won't. But at some point in his life, he will completely lose the ability to have a psychogenic erection.

This may sound like a terrible thing, but it's not. Remember, I didn't say that he couldn't have an erection, just not a psychogenic erection. He is going to need some form of physical stimulation of his penis in order to have erections. In basic terms, he's going to need foreplay, just the way his wife always has. Now remember, most men can't have an actual orgasm without some sort of physical stimulation, which they get either through masturbation or intercourse, so all this means is that this physical stimulation is going to have to start at an earlier phase so that he can get an erection in the first place. Where problems occur is when he doesn't know that this is a normal part of aging. But I'll get to that in a moment.

When men hear this, the first thing they want to know is at what age this will happen to them. That's a legitimate question, but it's also one I can't answer. Just as there were variations regarding when a man's refractory period would begin to lengthen, there are great variations regarding the age at which a man loses his ability to have a psychogenic erection. For some men it might occur as early as in their forties, while for others it might take place in their fifties, sixties, or even seventies. I can tell you that this will happen later in life to men who are in good cardiovascular shape, since it is blood being pumped into the penis that causes an erection. So in case you didn't have enough of an incentive to keep yourself in tip-top condition, this might do it. Do those men who still run marathons in their eighties and nineties and are in excellent cardiovascular shape still have psychogenic erections? I don't know, and I'm just as curious as you are, so if you know any and can get an answer, please tell me!

Penis Exercises

There's one more suggestion I'd like to introduce here. It has been shown that having an erection promotes a healthy penis. The blood that rushes into the penis when it is erect is full of oxygen, and that has been proven to be an important ingredient to maintaining a healthy penis. And when a penis is flaccid or limp, it is in a state of anoxia, or low oxygen supply.

Young men get erections all the time. In fact babies inside the womb have erections. As a man gets older, he has erections less frequently. If a man has reached the stage where he needs actual physical stimulation to get an erection, then he will have them even less often. But since erections promote good health in a penis, it follows that the more erections the better. So my advice to men who have lost the ability to have a psychogenic erection is to give yourself an erection from time to time.

It doesn't have to be only when your partner is around and you are going to have sex. Nor does it have to be that you are going to masturbate. Just think some sexy thoughts, or actu-

66

ally look at some erotic material if that is a necessary component of having an erection, even rub your penis through your clothes if that is appropriate to where you are, and cause an erection. Enjoy the feeling for a few moments, know that your penis is being revived with some vital oxygenation, and then let it go back down of its own accord. It certainly can't hurt you, and there's a good chance that these penis exercises will help maintain your penis in good physical shape.

Sexual Illiteracy

Case History: Ken and Vera

Ken first began to notice that something was different about his ability to become erect when he was fifty-two. Up until that point, when he saw his wife in the nude, he would start to get excited, and if he gave in to those feelings, his penis would become erect. But he started to notice that this cause-and-effect wasn't always happening. His wife had put on a few pounds in recent years and her breasts sagged a bit more than they had, and so he assumed that he was not as sexually attracted to her as he had been. By the time he was fifty-four, seeing his wife naked created absolutely no sensation in his penis, and as a result, he avoided having sex with her. Instead he would masturbate while looking at pictures of naked women that he downloaded from the web. Since he would begin touching his penis the moment he looked at the images, he never made the connection that the images themselves might not have given him an erection if he hadn't been creating the added sensory stimulation.

Returning to the loss of psychogenic erections, the biggest danger that arises from entering this phase comes not from the actual changes that are taking place but from what I call *sexual illiteracy*, in other words, sexual ignorance. For example, if a husband doesn't expect this change, he may think that the reason he's no longer having an erection when seeing his wife prance around naked is that she no longer arouses him. She's grown older too, and so her body has undergone some changes, and so he thinks that his lack of psychogenic erections is really her fault. He may even go out to seek greener pastures thinking that may help the situation.

Now I'm not going to tell you that a woman twenty years younger than this man's wife might not cause him to have renewed psychogenic erections. As a younger woman, her body may well be more attractive. And at the very least, she will present a change in scenery, and a little variety will always add stimulation. So with this new stimulation, he might find that his penis once again can stand up without any prodding. But the key question is: how long will this last? Sadly the answer is, not forever. After a certain time, the sight of this new woman isn't going to be enough to cause him to have an erection either because the problem isn't really about sexual stimulation, but blood flow. If his circulatory system isn't strong enough to pump sufficient blood into his penis, or if his veins aren't strong enough to keep the blood there after it has been pumped in, then he will still have erectile difficulties. So this man who went off in search of the fountain of youth will find himself erectionless with a new, younger woman, and she's not going to accept this situation as easily as would a wife of long-standing. If he had stayed with his wife, they would have had a much easier time, or at least should have had a much easier time, working through this change together.

I say would have, instead of should have, because in some cases sexual illiteracy plays havoc with the psyches of both parties. If she also didn't know about this coming change, she's going to say to herself either "He doesn't find me attractive anymore" or "He's giving at the office." In either case, instead of sympathy, she's going to give him the cold shoulder, which will only increase the chances that he's going to go looking elsewhere for sexual stimulation.

Let the Sun Shine In

Now that I've painted these black clouds for you, let's allow the sun to come out. Because you see, alleviating this situation is really no big deal. If she understands what is happening and is willing to take upon herself the duty of giving his penis the physical attention it needs, they can continue to have a very satisfying sex life. And, again, if their sex life had fallen into a rut, perhaps this change in formula may cause both of them to pay new attention to each other and to have a better sexual relationship than they'd had before.

This particular area is the perfect example of what I mean by manning your kayaks. The trick in this type of situation is to be nimble and make the necessary adjustments to these physical changes rather than allow yourself to be buffeted by the raging waters. Yes, he is the one undergoing physical changes regarding his erections, but the man and woman need to work as a team in order to overcome them. But if you desperately try to stay on that raft you were riding, at some point, one or both partners may just decide to jump ship.

And the Whitewater Years can definitely be a time of great sex. Yes, I know, younger people think that terrific sex only happens behind their bedroom doors, but the truth is, many couples have excellent sex lives during their Whitewater Years. Their relationship may be stronger, their skills better, and if they're working as a team, they can both enjoy sex as much or even more than they ever did before. As I said, the sun is still shining brightly despite all those clouds. You just have to maneuver yourselves so that it shines on you.

Further Changes

Of course as a man gets older, it will take more and more stimulation for him to get an erection, and the day may come that no matter what he tries, his penis won't rise to the occasion. If that day arrives, and it doesn't have to, we arrive at the term *impotent* or *erectile dysfunction*. As with the initial changes, this is unlikely to happen all at once, but after a certain period of starts and stops, he won't be able to get an erection the vast majority of times, if at all.

Up until a few years ago, a man had a few options, but they really weren't all that appetizing. Then along came Viagra (sildenafil citrate) and all that changed. But I'm jumping ahead of myself here, and we'll get back to Viagra in a bit.

At this point I want to tell you about some other changes to expect. As a man ages the force of his ejaculations are likely to diminish and the amount of the ejaculate may also lessen. So, in general, the entire experience of sex will cause much weaker sensations than it did when he was first entering sexual maturity in his teens. But as with the other changes I've mentioned, these changes too will be gradual and take many years to reach their final state.

I'm not going to say that all these changes are a good thing, and some men complain bitterly about the alterations to their sex lives. But if you adopt the right attitude, it doesn't have to be a calamity. And certainly no man should give up on having a sex life. I've taught men in their eighties who had given up on sex how to enjoy themselves. The results may not be as spectacular as when they were twenty, but I can assure you these men were quite satisfied. There's a saying, "act your age," and it does apply to sexual functioning. If you expect your sex life to be equal to what it was as a young man, you're undoubtedly going to be dissatisfied. But if you can learn to appreciate what you do have, you can still find a lot of joy in having sex because even a weakened orgasm is better than no orgasm at all.

Not Yet

As someone in his Whitewater Years, while you might have experienced the opening acts of some of these changes, basically I'm preparing you for what lies ahead, not especially what you might be facing now. As long as you don't overreact to what's happening, everything should be fine. But it is important to know what lies slightly further ahead because the better prepared you are psychologically, the better off you'll wind up. I'm fond of saying that the most important sexual organ lies not between your waist and your knees, but sits on top of your neck. That is to say, it's your brain that is most important when it comes to sex. So maintaining a proper attitude is key to retaining a healthy sex life.

Also, if you know that you are going to need more help than ever before in the near future from your wife, now would be the perfect time to make any repairs to your relationship so that when you're ready to start asking her for these new favors, she won't resent it.

One group of men who may find a real silver lining to all of this are those who never learned how to overcome premature ejaculation (PE). PE is a learning problem, not a physical one. Any man can train himself to recognize the premonitory sensation, that moment just before there is absolutely nothing he can do to prevent orgasm. Once he recognizes that moment, he can pull back from the edge, relax somewhat, and then keep going. In other words, he can control when he ejaculates. But for that group of men who never learned how to master this skill, the changes I've been speaking about can sometimes do the trick. All of a sudden they have control that they never had before, and without really trying. Because the need to have an orgasm isn't quite so strong, such men will develop the control they always sought and never found.

Erectile Dysfunction

The inability to obtain or maintain an erection is something that can strike a man of any age. Some young men have difficulties "getting it up" because they are worried about causing an unintended pregnancy. When a man loses a job he may become impotent, as a loss of his ability to support his family can temporarily damage his libido. And then there are diseases, like diabetes, or the treatments for other diseases, like chemotherapy, that can cause impotency. But the majority of men who face difficulties with their erections are older men. In other words, at some point in their lives, their refractory period becomes infinite and they just cannot become erect. (There are some common variations of impotency. Some men can become erect, but their erection isn't hard enough to allow for penetration. Other men become erect but then lose their erection either prior to penetration or just after they penetrate and then can't become erect again. In such cases, even though the man has an initial erection, he is still impotent, as he cannot have intercourse.)

Prior to the introduction of Viagra, men suffering from erectile dysfunctions had options, but they weren't all too pleasant. Doctors could insert a prosthetic device into a man's penis that either stayed firm or could be pumped up. Then the world of pharmacology developed an injection, which some men, for whom Viagra is not effective, still must use. Now don't get me wrong, such options were better than nothing for these men, but they did not represent the simplicity of taking a pill. But while Viagra is most definitely a major improvement, and there are others on their way to the market that may be even better, it is not a cure-all.

Viagra will give any man for whom it is appropriate an erection. (Men with certain conditions, particularly one that has to do with the heart or circulatory system, or who are taking certain medications—in particular short-acting nitrate drugs—should not take Viagra. I know that Viagra can be ordered illegally, and while you shouldn't do this because it is against the law, you most certainly shouldn't order and use Viagra unless your doctor has approved your use of it. Otherwise the punishment might be much more severe than a jail term.)

What Viagra won't give a man is sexual stimulation or desire. So if he's not sexually aroused to begin with, Viagra won't help him get an erection. To be sure, most men who are impotent are dying to have an erection, which is why so many of these little blue pills have been sold; and far too many illegally. But nevertheless, it is not an aphrodisiac.

As an aside, men who take Viagra do find that they may have erections at other times, such as during the night or in the morning, which they had stopped having. It has been shown that having an erection promotes a healthy penis because of the oxygen-rich blood that fills the penis, so it is quite possible that having erections caused by Viagra will cause the penis to become healthier and thus cause erections at other times as well. Whether or not Viagra could actually be used as a preventative measure against impotency has not been proved clinically.

Case Study: Ralph and Phyllis

Ralph was fifty-eight when he found that it was almost impossible for him to have an erection, no matter how hard he and his wife, Phyllis, tried. Without telling Phyllis, Ralph went to a urologist who prescribed Viagra. As soon as he left the doctor's office, Ralph stopped at a corner deli, bought a bottle of water, and took one of the pills. By the time he got home, he had a very strong erection. When he got inside their apartment, he walked over to Phyllis, took her hand and put it up against his trouser. She felt his erection and started bawling. Ralph didn't understand and started screaming at her, and that only made her more upset. He stormed out of the house without learning that Phyllis's best friend had just called her to say that she'd been diagnosed with breast cancer.

From my point of view as a therapist, the most important point to cover with regard to Viagra is that it is not a substitute for a good relationship. Just because the male half of a partnership has taken a pill doesn't mean that the female side wants to have sex at that very moment. So if a man needs to take Viagra to have sex, he must learn how to communicate with his spouse and fit this part of the dance of sex into their own pas de deux.

I have no doubt that this is going to be somewhat awkward in the beginning. Viagra forces couples to verbally communicate their desires ahead of time. But rather than being a negative, this may actually be a good thing. As I've been saying throughout this book, it promotes . . . now what's the word . . . that's right, intimacy!

There are many couples who never talk about sex. They get into the bed, the man reaches over and starts touching his wife, and if she responds positively, they have sex. If not, they roll over and go to sleep. Or maybe they always have sex on Tuesday and Saturday night, and so again, there's no need to talk about it. Is this a terrible thing? If they both get sexual satisfaction out of it, then the answer is no. When two people lead very busy lives, sometimes they have to "fit" sex into their schedule and really don't have the time for negotiations. But this type of routine is far from ideal. For one thing it's boring. And it's not very intimate.

So now you add Viagra to this mix. If the couple isn't communicating their desires verbally, and he needs to take a pill thirty minutes ahead of time, how is that going to work out? The answer is, it isn't. Viagra isn't like a condom that you can just slip on when it's needed. Viagra needs time to work so the only way that they are going to be able to successfully integrate Viagra into their love life is if they improve on their communications.

There are many problems that can arise from this situation. There are some wives who never enjoyed sex. Obviously something should have been done about this situation at the beginning of the relationship, but it was never taken care of. These wives were looking forward to the day that their husband's sexual demands would decrease or cease altogether. Then along comes this little blue pill and they feel that the sanctity of their bodies has been stolen from them. Pill or no pill, they're not going to want to cooperate.

A similar situation arises when the wife has been asking for changes in their love life, maybe for twenty or thirty years, and he was never willing to accommodate her desires. It might have been something as simple as giving her more hugs and kisses. Or it might have been some change in their sex routine that would have permitted her to have orgasms. Now after all these years, he's asking her for a favor. He needs her to agree to have sex with him at least thirty minutes ahead of time. How is she going to react to this request? All that pent up resentment is surely going to be exhibited in some form.

If a couple hasn't been on the same wavelength about sex and lovemaking in general, you don't have to be a seer or a sex expert to predict what is going to happen. Because Viagra isn't cheap, no man is going to risk taking one of those pills only to be rejected. He's going to want to make sure that she doesn't have a headache, or whatever. So he will be somewhat motivated to start things earlier than he ever did. He may start nuzzling her while she's doing the dishes, figuring that if she reacts positively, he has enough time to go take a pill so that by the time he gets her into bed, he has an erection. But she's not stupid. She's going to know what's going on and may react quite negatively because of it. She's going to say to herself: "He's not really interested in cuddling me and caressing me. All he wants is to see if he can have sex." If she rejects him at that point, he'll go off sulking, or maybe get angry, but it's certainly not going to lead to a wonderful evening of sex.

Of course for couples who have a good sex life and have been communicating their needs and desires and have been very attentive to each other as long as they've been together, the idea of having thirty minutes of foreplay while they wait for Viagra to work its magic will be no big deal because that's what they were doing before the husband needed chemical assistance. But there are many couples who may have started out all lovey-dovey and then fell into some sort of routine who will have some difficulties adjusting.

So for Viagra to work properly, the stage must be set as long in advance as possible. Ideally that should have been on their first date, but assuming that some problem areas exist, of whatever variety, the perfect time to begin making repairs is during the Whitewater Years. When the children were around, perhaps there was a good excuse for only having sex at bedtime and even for rushing a bit. But in an empty house, there's no reason not to hug or kiss or nuzzle earlier in the evening. I tell couples that foreplay for the next sexual episode starts the second after the end of the last one. That's one of the reasons that afterplay is so important. (For those of you who don't know what afterplay is, let me explain. A woman takes longer to become aroused, and it also takes her longer to come down from being aroused. So after a man and woman have had their orgasms, the woman still needs to be held and cuddled for a time. That's called afterplay, and as I said, afterplay sets up the foreplay of the next sexual episode, even if it's days away.)

So even though it's for selfish reasons, all you men out there in your Whitewater Years should begin adding as much romance to your relationship as you can in preparation for the day when that penis of yours is going to let you down. You'll have plenty of notice, because as I've pointed out, these changes appear gradually. So when you start feeling that your orgasms are changing; when you discover that you don't have an erection after seeing something sexually stimulating; when it takes you longer to become aroused for the next sexual episode, pay attention. These are signs that you're beginning to undergo some changes that may end up with the need to take Viagra and you don't want to have to deal with that at the last minute.

And even if you never need to use Viagra, once you get started with this romance thing, I believe you'll find that it has its own rewards. You'll end up having more sex, now that your schedules won't be quite as filled. Your overall relationship will improve, and that's important when you're spending more time together. And even when you're apart, let's say when you're off playing golf, if you've been giving your wife plenty of attention when you're around, she won't resent it as much.

One characteristic about intimacy is that it tends to go in one direction. If your relationship is clicking, then your level of intimacy can go up and up. But if you're both so busy that you don't find time for each other, then intimacy will quickly evaporate. And intimacy is not an emotion that just springs up, like those erections of yours. It needs nourishment and care. So start working on the intimate relations between you and your wife as soon as possible because if you wait until you're forced to, it might be too late.

Romantic Tips

For those of you who are clueless, let me give you some concrete tips on how to increase the amount of romance and intimacy in your life. The most important thing you can do is to listen to your wife. I don't mean just sit there and nod your head, but actually pay attention to what she is saying and respond appropriately. After all, that's what she's seeking the most—you. That's one reason women enjoy going out to dinner. It's an opportunity to spend some time together without the distractions of the telephone, the television, the children, and so forth.

Now of course women like presents, don't we all, but they should not substitute for your attention. If a husband is very busy and can't pay much attention to his wife, then she'll make do with a present now and then, but really, a few words, some time spent in your arms, and some passionate kisses will satisfy her a lot more than any present.

And when you're in bed making love, make certain that both of you are getting sexual satisfaction. Most women cannot have an orgasm from intercourse alone. These women need direct clitoral stimulation. In many cases, if they become sufficiently aroused during foreplay, they can have an orgasm from intercourse, but that's not true for every woman. Many can only have an orgasm if the man uses his finger, tongue, or even his big toe to stimulate her clitoris. If sex is a frustrating experience for a woman, you can be sure that she won't want to be extra helpful to her partner.

Psychological Issues

Case History: Jeff

Jeff was a salesman at a car dealership. He'd been earning a decent living, but then a large factory in the area closed and sales dropped dramatically. Not only were the workers who had been let go not buying cars, but neither was anyone else in town because of the fear of the possible effects this closing would have on other sectors of the economy. Since Jeff worked on commission, if he couldn't sell cars, he wasn't making any money. On top of that, his employer had a nasty temper, and with no customers in the showroom to force him to keep his cool, he was constantly exploding, and his salesmen were the usual objects of his wrath. Jeff and his wife, Kathy, generally had sex three or more times a week. But because of the atmosphere at work, Jeff just wasn't in the mood. After several weeks had gone by without having sex, Kathy was getting anxious. Not only was she needing the sexual release that came from having sex, but no matter how much Jeff told her that his lack of desire had nothing to do with her, she couldn't help feeling inadequate. Since Jeff didn't want to talk about it anymore, he withdrew into a shell and their entire relationship was suddenly on very rocky ground.

So far I've been speaking about the physical problems of aging as they relate to sex, but as you might imagine, there is a mental side to all of this too. When a man, of any age, has a problem obtaining or maintaining an erection, that can cause a vicious cycle to develop. For example, let's say a twenty-five-year-old man was chewed out by his boss that day. He goes home, worried that perhaps he'll lose his job, or is just dreading having to face his boss the next morning. His wife, on the other hand, has had a great day and she wants to celebrate by having sex that night. He doesn't turn her down, but all the worrisome thoughts going through his head weakens his libido, and though he would like to have an erection, his penis just won't cooperate. Given the circumstances it is understandable, and it would not happen the next time they try to make love, unless he worries about it happening again. When that occurs, a vicious cycle may develop. His worries about not having an erection cause him not to have an erection. What started out as a onetime occurrence now develops into a chronic problem.

I used that example to show that it can happen to a man of any age. But now let's look at a man of an older age. On a day when nothing special happened, he finds himself unable to have an erection. It's the start of the aging process that I've been telling you about. But it's only a minor incident and it could be years and even decades before it becomes serious, if at all. But like the first man, this man worries that it is going to happen again. And it will be those worries that ensure that it does. And before you know it, each time he tries to make love to his wife, his penis fails him and won't become erect. If he's heard anything about erectile dysfunction and aging (and with all the ads for Viagra on television, how could he not), he's likely to think, "This is it, I've reached the age where I'm impotent" when it is not "it" at all.

How can a man tell whether it's a mental block or real impotence? If you've been paying attention, then the answer should be evident. Age-related impotence does not occur overnight. There's a gradual diminishing of sexual prowess that takes years and years to reach possible impotence. I say possible, because while every man will have some deterioration of his sexual powers, not every man is destined to become impotent. So if a man can't have an erection one time, and from that time on he finds he can't have another one, then you can be almost certain that it's one of these mental vicious cycles that has caused the problem. Just knowing that it's not really impotence can be enough to sufficiently relax a man so as to allow him to regain his erections. But if he can't do it alone, then he should be able to accomplish his goal with the help of a sex therapist.

In such situations it is also very important that the wife be a willing partner in overcoming the problem. If a wife criticizes her husband for not being able to perform, that will only make his condition worse. Remember, the object in such cases is to get the man to relax. Any added tension will make it impossible for him to do that. What a sex therapist will sometimes do is ask the couple to engage in all sorts of sexual play but not allow them to have intercourse. If the man knows ahead of time that intercourse isn't in the picture, then he won't worry as much about not having an erection, and so hopefully will be able to have one. Once he regains confidence in his ability to have erections, he should be able to transfer that ability to a session when intercourse will take place. But his psyche will be delicate and if the wife doesn't play her role, then the problem may be all that more difficult to overcome. And by the way, when I say play her role, I mean just that. As I've said, she shouldn't be critical, nor should she act like too much of a cheerleader either. If she focuses his thoughts on his erections by giving him encouraging words, that could also cause a negative effect. The idea is to pretend as if there is no problem and hopefully, then, there won't be one.

There's something else that wives can do for their husbands, and that's to maintain a sexy image. As we saw, women who are entering their Whitewater Years have a tendency to put on a little weight, which is caused by the body's attempt to compensate for the loss of hormones. This change in appearance causes some women to want to cover up their bodies. Maybe they won't get undressed in front of their husbands as readily. Or they'll insist that the lights be turned off when they're making love or that they cover up under the sheets. The problem with such behavior is that men get aroused by visual stimuli, and if they're feeling a lack of confidence in their ability to become aroused, and their wives remove an important source of stimuli, a naked body, then it's going to make it that much harder for them to become aroused.

What's important to remember is that both of you are changing at the same time. If you both grow ashamed of your bodies and withdraw into a shell, then that's only going to make the situation worse. This is a time when you have to fight such urges and work at drawing each other out. Luckily, with the house empty of children and with more time on your hands and a little more money in your pockets, especially if you're finished paying for college tuitions, you can do something about it. You can go for some second honeymoons. Notice the plural form I've used. Even if it's just an overnight stay at a nearby bed-and-breakfast, the change of locale will help to encourage your libidos, and by charging your batteries now and again, you'll be able to keep going on the home front. You can try some different positions. You can make love in different rooms of the house. You can raid the refrigerator and cover yourselves with whipped cream or even caviar! The point is to do all you can to invigorate your sex life because you're at a stage that if you leave well enough alone, you might find yourselves left with nothing at all.

In some cases, an impotent man may be helped by taking doses, either injections or via a patch, of the male sex hormone, testosterone. However, studies have shown that in the vast majority of men, increasing the man's level of testosterone will not help him overcome impotency. Yet there are far too many physicians who offer men additional testosterone. An increased level of hormones, particularly in a man over the age of forty-five, could spread or promote growth of existing cancer cells. So if anyone ever suggests such a treatment to you for any reason, please be ultracautious and check with multiple physicians before proceeding.

CHAPTER 5

Other Male
Health Problems

THIS CHAPTER IS NOT GOING TO COVER ALL THE possible health problems that a male may encounter as he gets older. That would take an entire book and it's not within my competence in any case. What I want to cover here are conditions that will affect your sex life and your relationship. Some of these, like heart disease, for example, I did cover in chapter 3 on female health problems, but since there are some differences, I think the material is worth repeating, especially from a different perspective. And some problems, like prostate issues, were not touched on there.

Let me also stress right here that I'm not looking to depress you about the facts of older life, but rather prepare you so that you can live the rest of your life in the best way possible. In a sense the Whitewater Years are like the teenage years. During your teens you were preparing the way toward becoming an adult. Because of those changes, some people find their teen years to be quite tumultuous. In other words, they were another set of rapids that you had to get through in order to reach maturity. And how well you did set the tone for the rest of your life. If you got good grades and went to a good college, then you had an easier time than if you got poor grades and maybe didn't go to college at all. While no one will grade how you do in your Whitewater Years, the results will most definitely affect the ensuing stages of your life. For though you can't precisely control how your body ages, you do have some control regarding certain health issues, and you definitely have even more control of many of the psychological components. If you are properly prepared, it can definitely make the going a lot smoother. So smoothing out the bumps is what I have in mind for this chapter, not preventing them or making them go away. Sorry, but that's not within my power.

Going to the Doctor

I'm not in favor of stereotyping people, but sometimes a stereotype is just too common to ignore. The one I have in mind is that men don't go to doctors unless it's an absolute emergency. Some of this comes from the long-held view that a real man, a macho man, must always be stoic. Once you left the protection of your mother's apron, which these days means when you start school, if you fell and skinned your knee you were supposed to suck it up and not cry. Though it might take a few years, most boys learn that lesson very well, because if they don't, they are ostracized by the other boys and called a sissy. When these boys become men, going to the doctor can seem a bit like crying, and so they avoid it.

I think another component of this avoidance mechanism when it comes to medical treatment has to do with power. When you walk into a doctor's office and take off your clothes to be examined, you are most definitely not in the power position. That's especially true if part of the examination has you bending over. And while I never studied this issue, if you think about it, it probably has something to do

with your penis too. Some men might be afraid that their penis is too small and would prefer to keep it inside their pants.
Others might be afraid of getting an erection. But whatever
the components of this attitude, the bottom line is that men
are a lot more reluctant to go to the doctor than women are.

I don't have the training to tell you why this is not a good
idea when it comes to medical matters such as heart disease,
though common sense would tell you that the sooner you begin to treat a condition, the easier it will be and the greater
the chance of success. Where I can comment is when it
comes to issues of sexuality and relationships. As I already
said, when I gave sessions at a clinic in the Department of
Gerontology at New York University Hospital, men in their
eighties came to me finally admitting that they hadn't had
any sexual enjoyment for a decade or more. In many cases,
I was able to turn that situation around, and this was long
before the invention of Viagra, and boy were they delighted!
Had they come earlier, they would have had that pleasure
much, much sooner. And I know there are countless other
men who never go for help and so spend their final decades
without sharing in the joy of sex.

Now Viagra has definitely reduced that number, and
that's great, but look how many men are buying their Viagra
over the Internet rather than being checked out by their doctor first, running the risk of serious complications. Some
may do it to avoid the cost of a visit, but I'm willing to bet
that most do it to avoid the embarrassment. (And here I'm
only talking about older men who require Viagra. I know
that there are plenty of younger men who are taking it for
other reasons, such as to overcome the effects of certain
drugs on their ability to have an erection, for which no doctor would give them a prescription.)

So how do I convince you, if you fall into that group of
men who shy away from the doctor's office, to go for regular

checkups? The only way I can think of is to explain how it can affect your present and future sex life.

As I explained in the chapter on women's health, a person who survives a heart attack can usually have sex, but many don't because they're afraid that it might cause another one. Now the best way to avoid this situation is to take care of that ticker so that you don't get a heart attack in the first place. Some of what you can do is within your control, like getting enough exercise and eating properly, but to really ensure that your heart is working properly, you need a doctor's expertise.

But no matter how you control your lifestyle, and no matter how good your doctor may be, for some individuals with a genetic predisposition to heart disease, heart trouble is unavoidable. Now if you fall into that category, or if you've already had some form of heart disease, then in order to maintain your sex life, the key will be open communication with your spouse. You have to be able to work as a team to get the answers you need from your physician, and then you have to come up with a sexual game plan that will maximize the sexual satisfaction you both get while minimizing the strain on your heart. So you see the bottom line is, either you learn to work with the medical community or there's a good chance that your sex life will go "poof." If that doesn't convince you, then I'm not sure what will. But since I don't give up easily, here's some vital information aimed at those of you who do go to the doctor on a regular basis, as well as those who are more likely to see a doctor in an emergency room than on a scheduled visit.

Poor Blood Flow

An erection is physically achieved by increased blood flow into the penis. Any disease that decreases a man's blood flow can affect his ability to have an erection. Among the diseases that can have this effect are hardening of the arteries (arteriosclerosis), diabetes, and high blood pressure (hypertension).

Since these disorders also carry more serious consequences, they must be treated, whether or not they cause a man any erectile problems. If you're going to avoid treatment for these dangerous conditions, then really there's no hope for you. But let me point out that it's quite possible that a sudden problem with being able to obtain erections could well be a symptom of one of these diseases. So having erectile difficulties is absolutely something that you should mention to your doctor because in trying to get to the bottom of your inability to have an erection, your doctor might discover one of these dangerous underlying conditions, and that could be a lifesaver.

Case History: John

When John went for a physical at age fifty-four, his doctor reported back to him that his blood pressure was on the high side. He prescribed some medicine to bring it down, which John took as directed. When John first heard the news about his elevated blood pressure, he had become somewhat nervous. His doctor had mentioned to him that one side effect of the drug he would be taking might be some difficulties in obtaining an erection, but the words hadn't sunk in. A few weeks later, when he began to experience some erectile dysfunction, he never connected it with the drug. He thought it was just one more sympton of growing older, like his high blood pressure.

Side Effects of Medicine

If you happen to have a problem with your circulation, then your doctor is going to prescribe some sort of medication to correct it. All medications have side effects, though not every person taking a particular medication will experience them. A common side effect of medications that affect blood flow is erectile difficulties. Your doctor should warn you of this beforehand, but as I've said, some doctors remain skittish when it comes to discussing matters having to do with sex. Also, if a doctor warns you that a drug may cause you to become impotent, and you then worry about it, you could suffer the consequences not because of the drug, but because of those worries.

But medications that correct blood flow are not the only ones that can affect your ability to have an erection. There is a long list of medications that may prevent a man from having erections including: antidepressants, sedatives, anti-anxiety agents, narcotics, hormones, drugs for peptic ulcers, stimulants, tranquilizers, and even some over-the-counter medications for colds or allergies.

The key to handling this risk is to watch for cause and effect. If you start taking a particular medicine and suddenly develop problems with obtaining or maintaining your erection, then bring it up to your physician. Whatever you do, don't merely stop taking the medication to restore your erections. That could be quite dangerous. There's a good chance that another drug, made to handle the same condition, won't cause you this particular side effect and so your doctor, who knows about such things, can hopefully solve this problem quite easily. But if you stop taking medication, your erections might return, but the underlying condition will undoubtedly worsen, and in the end that could leave you in very bad shape, both in terms of your sex life and your health.

Case History: Waiter

I went on the *Larry King Show* one time and spoke about the need for men to examine themselves for testicular cancer.

A few months later, I was in a restaurant when one of the waiters pulled me aside. He told me that he had seen me that night, examined his testicles, found something wrong, and gone to the doctor. It turned out to be cancer, and because he caught it early enough, he was fine. I've actually had a few other men tell me similar stories since then.

The moral of this story is that rather than ignore any signs of a health related problem, you should go out of your way to look for them, including examining your testicles, much as women examine their breasts, because the earlier you detect cancer, the better the odds that you will survive and even thrive.

Prostate Cancer

The most common form of cancer that hits men is cancer of the prostate. There are several ways of treating this form of cancer, including surgery to remove the prostate, radiation, which can take the form of inserted pellets, and hormonal therapy. No matter which type is used, the likelihood is that the man will become impotent. There are some changes on the horizon, including surgical procedures that don't damage the nerves that cause erections, but for the moment, the odds are that impotency is going to occur.

Viagra may help some of these men, depending on the exact treatment that was used, and some of the other methods, including the injection method, may also work. Whatever fears of impotence you may have regarding this terrible disease, put them aside, particularly because the sooner you are treated, the less damage there will be and the greater the likelihood that your ability to have erections can be restored.

Other Prostate Problems

While it's a sad statistic that 40,000 men die of prostate cancer in the United States every year, the vast majority of prostate problems are benign. The prostate is a walnut-sized organ that surrounds the urethra, the tube that descends from the bladder and runs through the penis. This gland produces the whitish liquid that forms the bulk of semen. This organ can become infected, but that's generally a short-term issue solved by drugs. But as men age, their prostate glands tend to grow larger. This larger prostate squeezes the urethra, making it more difficult for a man to urinate, and in some cases, impossible, though the most common problem is a frequent urge to urinate. How common? It affects more than half of all men in their sixties and in older men it is thought that as many as 90 percent are affected. So it's almost inescapable that this condition, known as benign prostatic hypertrophy (BPH), will affect you at some point down the road.

There are many different modalities of treatment, from drugs to surgery, and some can cause impotency. The earlier the symptoms of BPH lead you to seek medical assistance, the less likely that a radical treatment, most likely to cause impotency, will be needed. So once again, the key is to mention any changes that you might have with respect to urination to your doctor as soon as possible. And if you don't, if you let the situation fester, I can almost guarantee that it's going to play havoc with your sex life eventually. You're going to worry about it, you're going to worry that you might become impotent, and those worries alone can prompt impotency to occur. So rather than pretend nothing is wrong and risk losing it all, go to see your doctor and hopefully you can successfully battle this condition.

Pain from Arthritis and Other Causes

One of the consequences of growing older is more frequent aches and pains. The older you get, the more likely you are to pull or sprain some muscle or other, and it also takes longer for these problems to heal. Your back may have developed a tendency to go out. Or your joints may hurt, either from wear and tear or arthritis. Pain, which was something you rarely thought about before, becomes a part of your life—either dealing with it or trying to avoid it.

If you have turned into a couch potato over the years, then sex may be one of the more physically active items on your agenda. And so not only might you have to deal with an existing pain when having sex, but you also might be afraid of causing yourself a painful injury. The obvious solution is to make some compromises, and the biggest one shouldn't be giving up on sex.

If a man has an arthritic shoulder or wrist, he is going to have problems holding himself up in the male superior or missionary position. And if a man feels pain of any sort, that may well cause him to lose his erection, especially if his erection is on the weak side to begin with. But just because one position has to be removed from the bedroom playbook doesn't mean that the game has to be forfeited. That will only happen if the couple is not communicating. If he won't admit what the problem is, then he might avoid having sex. But if he feels comfortable telling his wife that he can't use the position they've always used because he knows that his wife will agree to try some other positions, then all will be well.

There are also going to be couples for which intercourse may not be possible at all. They may not be able to find a position that allows both of them to be comfortable enough for the man to insert his penis into her vagina and for both of them to move around. Again, this doesn't necessarily have to spell the end of their sex lives. Each partner can probably find a position that is comfortable during which he or she can give the other person an orgasm, using either the hand, the tongue, or a vibrator.

Starting Early

Of course if a couple has never performed oral sex, it is going to be somewhat harder to start when they're seventy-five, say. Especially if it's under the pressure of not being able to have sex the way they've always been used to. That's why I would suggest if a couple has never experimented with different positions that the Whitewater Years are the years to begin the process. Let me give you an example of why this is so.

Let's say a wife has never performed oral sex on her husband. If she is hesitant, one suggestion I might make to a couple would be for her to kiss and lick his penis for a minute or so, just to get used to the sensations and tastes, and then switch to their normal sexual routine to reach orgasm. Eventually she might progress to the point of giving him an orgasm through oral sex, but she won't feel pressured into having to if she has the means she always had to fall back on. But if the normal routine is suddenly out of the picture, there is going to be a dramatic difference in the psychology of any early experimentation. He's going to desire an orgasm. He's not going to appreciate it if she suddenly stops. And the very fact that she is under pressure is going to make it even more likely that she won't like the experience. Instead of feeling positive about what she is doing, she will feel like she is under the gun. That's going to cause her level of arousal to sink like a stone, and being aroused is important to enjoying any sexual activity. So here's a case where the timing that is most likely to lead to success will be to start any such experimentation during your Whitewater Years.

This applies for just about any new position. If a woman has never gone on top of her lover, she may feel awkward the first time. It may take a while to figure out exactly how to have him place his penis inside of her vagina. If she's still quite nimble, that shouldn't be much of a problem. And if a couple has been having sex in the female superior position for some time, they will probably be able to continue as they get older because they've had a lot of practice, and they have the confidence that comes from experience. Also, she'll have figured out why this position is so pleasing to her, so she'll have the incentive to find ways to accommodate any changes in her body so that this position still works for her. But if an older couple were to first try such a position and run into any difficulties, they'd be more likely to give up.

And then there are the psychological issues. Older people tend to be more set in their ways. They don't particularly like to experiment. That doesn't apply to every older person, but it certainly is true of many. They'll automatically say, "You can't teach an old dog new tricks." Now I happen to know that that's not true. I'm always trying new things. But many older people don't feel that way.

But you're not at that stage yet, and if your Whitewater Years are going to be vital ones, you have to be willing to try new things. You have to visit new places, taste new foods, play different sports, read new authors, and experiment with new sexual positions. If you keep this positive attitude going, then you'll never fall into one of those ruts. And you'll be positioning yourselves to maintain that open attitude toward new things until the end of your days.

Taking Care of Yourself

Another psychological issue has to do with appearance. If you look into the mirror and say to yourself, "Who is that old guy?" that can certainly lower your self-esteem, which in turn can lower your desire for sex. So as you age, it's more important than ever to take care of that body of yours. It may be too late to emulate Mr. America, but you can certainly aim for any needed improvements.

When you're young you may take your body for granted, but once you start seeing changes, that's when you have to tell yourself that it's time to take some action. A certain amount of sagging and shrinking does take place as various body parts start to age. But you can counter that effect by building muscle. Not only will you feel better, but you'll also be able to minimize some of the physical changes. (This is an advantage that men enjoy over women, who, while they too benefit from exercise and can improve their tone, will find it harder to build new muscles.) If you develop your back and shoulder muscles, you won't slouch and that will keep you from appearing shorter, even if you do lose an inch or so. In fact, if you've been someone who's always slouched, by making some improvements to your posture, you can actually look taller. And while women have a greater risk of developing osteoporosis, a thinning and weakening of the bones, men too can suffer from this condition, and regular exercise can help both sexes strengthen and rebuild their bones. And when you don't exercise, your muscles begin to atrophy, which worsens your condition. And if your muscles become too weak to support you, you can develop difficulties walking or even maintaining your balance.

An Ounce of Prevention

Exercise has other preventative aspects as well. Aerobic exercise slows or prevents the buildup of cholesterol plaque in the veins and arteries and also can keep your arteries more flexible, which helps to prevent hardening of the arteries and high blood pressure. Exercise also improves the functioning of the liver, pancreas, and other vital organs. And because aerobic exercise helps your body metabolize sucrose, it can help you to control diabetes. Exercise also increases your body's production of human growth hormone, which decreases as we age, and which helps to maintain the size and strength of your muscles.

It Can Get Bigger or Smaller

And then let me add one more reason having to do with a part of the body that I specialize in. Many men develop a potbelly after a certain age. They may think it's inevitable, but it's not. I'm not saying that you need a "six-pack" on your stomach to be happy, but you also don't want to have a beer belly either. Certainly having a large belly protruding from right above where your genitals are located is not going to make having sex any easier. And if you do develop too much of a belly, you might not realize another effect that this has; it makes your penis appear smaller. While two-thirds of your penis is visible, one-third is buried beneath the skin. If a man gains weight, that ratio changes as more and more of his penis disappears under layers of fat. So an older man who thinks that the aging process has shrunk his penis may really only be experiencing a visual effect that is the result of added poundage. In other words, his penis hasn't shrunk but rather a part of it has gone into hiding. You can keep this from happening merely by being careful about the size of your middle.

What to Do and How to Do It

What type of exercise routine should you develop? You must consult with your doctor because whatever you do must be within your physical possibilities, but a good routine will include strength training, that is to say exercise with weights, as well as aerobic exercise to build your heart, lungs, and keep your blood vessels open. You may read articles that say walking is a great form of exercise and that's true. But remember, walking isn't enough because it only works the lower half of your body. You don't want to neglect any major muscle groups, so ask your doctor to give you some guidelines.

One important side of exercise is maintaining the incentive to keep going week in and week out, for if there are large gaps in your exercise schedule, you'll barely be able to maintain a certain level of fitness; certainly not increase it. One way of doing that is to use the buddy system. If one part of a team doesn't feel like doing whatever is on the schedule, the other partner can generate the necessary push to get them going. And if you're married, then you have a built-in exercise partner, that person who is sharing your bed.

When you were younger, it may have been true that your wife wasn't a suitable exercise partner. As a young man you could probably outperform her in many areas. You may have found it frustrating to wait for her to catch up or to lower yourself to her level. (This is obviously not true for every couple, but is with many couples.) But as the years have gone by, there's a good chance that the disparity has narrowed. And let's face it, you may no longer be up to playing singles tennis or full-court basketball. By taking up biking, doubles tennis, speed walking, or roller blading, you can definitely share the joys of these activities while also giving each other the support to keep it up. And the time you spend together will undoubtedly enhance your romance as well.

Dr. Ruth's Pet Peeves

I'm often asked about sex as a form of exercise, with people wanting to know how many calories are burned and so forth. My attitude about that is that it is a ridiculous question. If you're busy thinking about how many calories you're burning while you're making love, then you're not concentrating on the important aspects of what you are doing. So if there are some extra benefits to your health from having sex, look at them as bonus points, but definitely don't include the time you're having sex as counting for your total minutes of exercise for the week. And I share these same views regarding the caloric content of the male ejaculate, which people often ask me about as well. I think it's absurd, and bad manners, to count calories when you've accepted an invitation to someone's home for dinner, and ten times so to start calculating calories while performing oral sex.

Getting Out Those Kayaks

Throughout this book I've been making the analogy to kayaks. I'm sure many of my male readers like that image because many men enjoy pitting themselves against Mother Nature in the great outdoors. But as I brought up in the beginning of this chapter, when it comes to matters of their health, they will often put their tail between their legs and run the other way. That this phenomenon exists, there is no doubt, and I already speculated a bit on why it does. But the important issue for you is to figure out how to avoid this trap.

I chose as a first line of attack to give you information about the changes that you can expect, and to link them as best I could to your sexuality. Men are universal in their fear of losing their ability to have sex. I don't think this has anything to do with the so-called castration complex. A man's testicles may pal around with his penis, but men don't really think about their testicles that much nor connect them with sex in any conscious way. It's the penis that is the body part that they associate with sex, and it is the penis, which often acts as if it had a mind of its own in any case, that they want to keep as healthy as possible.

But as I've shown, now that you're in your Whitewater Years, the manner in which your penis functions from now on is going to be directly related to how the rest of your body is doing. If your blood flow is poor, if you're taking certain medications, if you're afraid of causing damage to your heart, then your penis is not going to perform properly, at least not in the sexual arena. So to follow your normal pattern when it comes to your health, that is to say to ignore any symptoms unless they reach a critical point, is going to have some unwanted repercussions below your belt.

Case History: Frank

Frank played football in college. He had damaged his knee when he was a junior, but he never let it get the best of him; he managed to play all through his senior year despite the pain. After college, the knee would give him trouble now and then, but nothing that he couldn't handle. But when he entered his Whitewater Years, his knee really began to act up. But since he'd never let it get him down before, he refused to give in to the pain. He obviously needed surgery, but he wouldn't go to the orthopedist. The problem was that while he stubbornly refused medical help, he also was forced into a more and more sedentary life, one that his wife resented, as hiking was one of her favorite activities. They would argue over this constantly, and it began to have a negative impact on their relationship.

Giving Him Help

They say a tiger can't change his stripes, and that's true. Yes an older man may go to the doctor more often because he's forced to by a series of different chronic problems; but if his attitude doesn't change, it may not help him all that much. If he's told to watch what he eats but ignores the doctor's advice. If he's given medications but fails to take them. If he is put on an exercise regime and skips it most days. If he's told to cut down his intake of alcohol but doesn't. If he ignores the doctor's advice as much as possible, then he may as well not have gone in the first place.

So how does a man learn to make the necessary adjustments to growing older? I think a good part of the answer is through teamwork with his wife. Perhaps psychologically he can't give in to this new dependency on the medical establishment, but he can give in to his wife's prodding because, after all, she loves him and he has given in to her in so many other ways over the years.

I know there are wives who say this is silly. Why should they have to take on the responsibility for his health? "What's the matter with him," they say, "is he a baby?" That's one way of looking at it, but there is another. When you were both younger, he was your hero. If there was trouble, you ran into his arms for protection. Consciously or not, you fed the notion that he was your he-man. So can you really expect him to suddenly throw off that title and meekly admit that his body is failing him?

"But isn't he afraid of his heart failing or his arteries clogging?" Isn't a man afraid of attacking a hill full of enemy soldiers? Of course he is, but he's been trained, from those early days in grade school when he learned the lesson not to cry, that a man doesn't give in to his fear. Now it's not that he's afraid of what the doctor might do; he's afraid of what the doctor might find. He's afraid that his manhood may somehow not be there in quite the same strength it was before. And that's the type of fear he's been trained to thrust aside and ignore.

I'm simplifying here, but my point is, in this particular arena, a man may need to lean on some of the particular strengths of his wife. Women are better at cooperation, and that includes cooperating with their doctors. As you enter this new phase together, women should use the relationship they have with the medical community to lead their husbands through this set of rituals. This is not an area where she should stand her ground. She shouldn't cut off her nose to spite her face and say, "If he won't make an appointment to go to the doctor, I'm not going to make it for him" or "If he won't take his medicine, that's his problem." Look, if he gets sick, it's going to be your problem, too, believe me. If he requires your help, give it to him without question. And if he needs some prodding, then prod. The Whitewater Years are going to bring all sorts of changes to your lives. You're going to have to reassess over and over and over again. Here's a case where if you're needed to take the lead role as far as the health of both of you is concerned, then just do it. Nobody wins if you sit it out on the sidelines while his health deteriorates.

And you men, maybe you need a nudge to go to see your doctor, and as you see I'm willing to stick up for you and ask your wives to help you, but you have to cooperate too. You can be a little stubborn for show, but then you have to give in and get the medical attention you require. There's only so much your wife can do, and while it's true that she too will in some way suffer from any illnesses you may get, you'll suffer a whole lot more.

CHAPTER **6**

Empty-Nest Syndrome

THERE ARE MANY COUPLES WHO SAY THEY can't wait until the day that all their children have left home. Perhaps you've seen the television commercial for Disney World where the parents pack off their daughter for college, and the moment she's gone, they jump for joy and head for Disney World. Well, there's fantasy, there's Madison Avenue, and there's reality. And the reality is that most parents, not all but most, are downright miserable when a child goes off to college. And if it's the last child, with no more offspring at home, the effect can be multiplied.

Having said that most parents aren't happy to see their children leave them, I must also say that this is the short-term effect. No matter how miserable those first few days, weeks, or even months may be, the ache will slowly disappear. And when they first come home from college, and bring with them their mess, their noise, their appetites, and their dirty laundry, even the parents who shed the most tears in September may actually be glad to see them go off again after the holidays.

There are many stages in life that require a need to mourn, and facing a house devoid of children is definitely one of them. But a mourning period doesn't last forever, and if the parents have a healthy relationship, that's all this time will be—a mourning period—not a permanent crisis. But if there were cracks in their relationship, cracks that they may not have even been aware of, then the departure of their children could have much more serious consequences.

I'm going to give you some tips on how to cope with your children leaving home, but in reality, that's not my definition of empty-nest syndrome. Instead I might label that transitional period empty-nest flu, because like the flu it's going to make you miserable for a time, but there's nothing much that you can take for it and you will get better. But when serious underlying problems in a relationship surface after the kids have left, then you have what I consider to be empty-nest syndrome. And I have to report some bad news regarding this condition: not every relationship is going to survive. In some cases, the existing damage will be too far along to make repairs. It's like a house that has been abandoned for too many years. It's better to tear it down and start again then try to restore it because the structure is no longer sound.

If a husband and wife still have a few years until their nest is totally empty, and if they sense that their relationship may be on rocky ground, then I would urge them to begin working on that relationship right away. The best thing they could do is to go for marital therapy, but at the very least they should begin trying to reconnect and solidify their relationship on their own. I'll deal more with this a bit further on.

Case History: Joe and Janet

Joe had a drinking problem. Every night he'd come home from work and have several drinks then fall asleep in front of the TV. His wife, Janet, would try to get him to talk to her or interact in some way, but there was nothing she could do or say that would keep him sober. While the kids were around, she suffered through this, for at least Joe was able to hold onto his job and bring home a weekly paycheck. But when the kids had moved out and Janet was left alone with a drunken husband in the living room every night, she decided that she'd had enough and left him.

The Danger Is Real

I'm sure there are many couples who will deny that these risks are as severe as I am painting them. They may know that they have problems, but they figure that the opposite will happen; when the children are gone, they'll finally have the time to heal the rift and repair their relationship. It's true that sometimes pressure—and the hectic life of having to work and raise children is certainly a pressure cooker—is a prime source of stress, and when the pressure is released, the stress will dissipate and a solution can be arrived at. But that's not always the case.

Let's demonstrate why I'm saying this with a sad physical example. There are accidents where the victim gets trapped between two hard objects, for example, someone falls between a moving train and the platform. The victim remains conscious and the rescue workers talk to that person as they're working, but from experience they know that this is only temporary. The moment that the victim is released from the pressure of the trap he or she is in, the blood will pour out of them and that person will die.

Now let me give you a relevant example of the negative effects that a childless environment can have as it relates to empty-next syndrome. Take a couple where one spouse always works late. It's not that this person has to spend so many hours away from home, but he or she prefers not to have to go home. The other spouse takes refuge in the fact that he or she isn't alone at night because there are children around who make some noise, provide some company, and keep him or her occupied by asking for help with their homework or needing their clothes washed, and so forth. They rationalize that their marriage is viable because everyone is working so hard to maintain the family. Then the children leave. The source of the pressure has disappeared. The spouse who is stuck at home no longer has company or an excuse to keep busy. The silence becomes deafening.

Not every marriage in which this occurs ends, but that's not because it shouldn't. The marriage may continue, but the relationship is in fact dead. At least one-half of this couple doesn't want to see the other half. And the other half will soon start to resent it and their love may well turn to hate.

It can certainly be stressful to care for children, but it should not overwhelm the relationship of the parents. (Obviously if a couple has very many children, or a sick child, or some other aggravating factor, taking care of children can be overwhelming.) When it does, it often means that the parents are hiding the truth behind this excuse. In other words, they may not have gone out for a romantic dinner together in years, but the reason they give isn't that they would feel uncomfortable but that they can't leave the children alone, even if their children are teens who aren't around at dinnertime anyway.

I regularly see couples in my private practice who are in just such a predicament. Now I think I'm a pretty good therapist and I've helped lots of couples get back together, but when I'm faced with one of these scenarios, I know that I've got a very big challenge in front of me, and that more often than not, I am going to fail. The main reason is that years and even decades may have passed while they lived under this illusion that it was the pressure of having children that kept them from acting romantic toward each other. When the kids do leave, the romance doesn't revive because it's long gone and buried. There's nothing left to resurrect. They may once have loved each other, but in the intervening years the two partners have gone in absolutely different directions and never the twain shall meet. Quite often, at least one of the spouses actually hates the other. This is an absolutely hopeless situation.

You often hear of couples staying together for the sake of the children, and so when the children have left, they should leave each other. Some do and some don't, but just because they live under the same roof doesn't mean that there is any relationship left. And, in my opinion, once the kids are gone, this type of couple is better off splitting up. In the first place, one or both may find a new partner and resume getting the love and attention he or she deserves. But even if they don't, they'll have removed a constant source of irritation, their spouses.

Is It Better to Be Alone?

While some couples stay together for the children, they will also stay together after the children have left the nest. The reason is a combination of shame (regarding their friends and relatives as well as their children), laziness, and convenience. She may be afraid that she will never find another partner and so prefers to be able to say she's married, while he may like having a built-in housekeeper. Or they both might work and are so involved with their work that they don't want to be bothered going through a divorce and the ensuing search for a new partner.

These people have either forgotten what it's like to be in love or purposefully pushed those thoughts aside. But to go through the rest of your life with an empty hole where your heart was, and to have a rotten or nonexistent sex life, is just not the right way to close out your days. Yes, going through a divorce can be an anguish-filled process, and it can be difficult to find a new partner, but if you can meet someone new there's really no better satisfaction. There are many lonely people in the world who would love to have a partner, and here this group gives up without even trying.

Of course, there are many people in this group that end up having affairs, possibly even before the children have departed. At least that spouse is getting some emotional and physical gratification, but the original relationship is battered even further.

Is there a way to tell where your relationship stands? If the proper description of your lives is that of two ships passing in the night, does that mean that it is nothing more than a ghost? Not necessarily. We live in a different world. When both husband and wife work outside the home, it can be very difficult to keep a relationship bubbling. So the question is not one of quantity but quality. You're not spending as much time together as a couple as you want or should, but when you are together, are you happy? Is it a relief to fall into each other's arms for even five minutes, or is it something that you've start avoiding? When you think of your partner during the day, does it give your spirit a lift or does it merely make you angry? Do you share your life with your partner or do you only share your children's lives? When you're walking down the street, or at the mall, or on the sidelines of your kids' games, do you reach for each other's hands, or do you put them in your respective pockets? There are a million little signs that show whether your relationship is healthy or if it is strained or actually hurting. Don't ignore them, and if a majority are pointing in the wrong direction, do something about them.

Once again I've painted a bleak picture and I apologize. But in a country where about 50 percent of all marriages end in divorce, I'd be remiss not to point out the rocky shoals. Putting your head in the sand the way ostriches are said to do is not going to save your marriage. At best it will postpone the inevitable. But there is a point where a marriage can still be saved, and I'm hoping that by alerting you to the possibility, you'll do something before it's too late.

Cures for Empty-Nest Flu

There is going to be some pain when the kids leave. I remember turning a corner at Princeton University after having said goodbye to my son and sobbing like a baby. Talk to any mother who's gone through that experience and you're likely to be told that tears were involved. And if fathers don't all cry, they certainly share in the pain.

Now those tears represent a mixture of emotions. In part they're for your child and the fears you have for leaving him or her to fend for him- or herself. They're also for the loneliness that you're feeling at not having this precious person by your side. And they're for the fact that a certain stage of your life is over, and that you're a lot older than when it began eighteen years ago.

Of course, your child is going to be fine, and that will calm those fears. And not only will you get used to not having this child around as often, but in this day and age you'll also find yourself communicating a lot, maybe even more than when they lived under your roof. When my son was at Princeton I had to hope to find him in his room when I called, and then had to worry how much the call was costing me. These days most college students have a cell phone with unlimited minutes on nights and weekends for long distance calls so you won't have to worry about the cost of phone calls, and since they'll always have their phones with them, you will be able to reach them no matter whether they're in their rooms or not. And while my son and I would exchange occasional letters, with email and Instant Messaging, you'll be sending messages back and forth at all times of the day and night. In other words, staying in touch is not a problem.

So the main, long-term problem has little to do with your offspring, but with you. And you can choose to wallow in your misery or to start moving on with your life. That is to say, climb into your kayaks and start paddling!

With your children out of the house, you're going to have more free time, both in terms of actual minutes and how to use those minutes. First there are those newfound minutes. Instead of doing six or more loads of laundry a week, it will drop to one or two. And once you neaten up the house, it will stay neat. There will be a lot less dirt tracked into the house. You'll spend less time hunting for things the kids misplaced. And as to scheduling, as opposed to kids being starved and wanting dinner early, you can now have a leisurely cocktail before dinner and eat later. Or make love before the eleven o'clock news. Or start a jigsaw puzzle and leave it on the table undisturbed for a week.

Whatever you do, don't fritter away those newfound minutes. Instead of watching more television, watch less. Don't offer those minutes up to your job by working longer hours every night. Instead put aside time to do things for yourself, and do things together with your partner. And to do that, you have to have a game plan. You have to talk about what it is you might want to do together, and set aside the time to do it.

Case History: George and Helen

Helen loved soap operas. Though she worked in an office, she had her VCR set every day to tape four of them.

Right after dinner, she'd go off into the living room to catch up on what had happened to her favorite characters. Even though they were on tape, to Helen watching the shows was like a religion and she never skipped a night. Her husband, George, worked in a noisy factory where conversation was just about impossible. He would have liked to spend some time discussing things with his wife, but her evenings were all tied up. After the kids left home, George started going to the corner bar every evening just so that he'd have some companionship. He met a woman there, whose husband was addicted to watching sports, and they began an affair.

Doing Away With Boredom

From my experience as a therapist, I can tell you that one of the most dangerous pitfalls of any marriage is boredom. Communication is important, but if you are saying the same things over and over to each other, or only dealing with mundane items that you'd rather not hear about for the umpteenth time, then that's going to put the kibosh on further communication. You'll find yourselves avoiding talking altogether. Sex is great but if it's the same old same old then it's going to get old very quickly. Just as you wouldn't want to eat the same meal every night for dinner, no matter how much you enjoyed it the first time, so too you need to inject some variety into every aspect of your lives.

Let me stress that this is a very important point and that it will take some effort on both your parts to keep boredom at bay. I'm not against routines and it's really not important whether you take your shower in the morning or at night. My main concern is that you both have things to say to each other that will make for interesting conversation. Something you did twenty years ago and you've spoken about fifty times can't help but be boring. Save the old stories for your future grandchildren. You need to start making new legends. It's something that I want you to always keep in mind, but especially when following some of the suggestions I'm about to make. If you're constantly in search of ways to make your lives more interesting, you'll have more interesting lives. But if you don't bother, then boredom will set in, and when the cobwebs start to cover your relationship and your romance, that's not a healthy sign.

Some Suggestions

I'm going to go into more detail in chapter 10, but I want to give you a few recommendations at this point just to illustrate my point.

My first general suggestion is to find some activities that will take you away from the old homestead. You could drive around the country looking at antiques. Or visit relatives you haven't seen in a while. Or take in a minor league baseball game in some town a few hours away. Or go skiing. Or even prance around naked at a nudist camp.

There are a number of reasons that I'm suggesting you get away from the home front. One is that without the kids, it's now a lot easier and cheaper to pull together, so if you've been sticking close to home all these years, use this opportunity to travel a bit. You'll be building new sets of memories that will reward you for years to come. And then at home there are reminders of your children, which you won't have when away, as well as reminders of chores to do, though without kids you'll see that your home to-do list will get shorter and shorter.

Playing by Vacation Rules

When it comes to sex, and you know in one of my books I'm going to get to that subject again and again, many people find it more exciting to have sex away from their own bedroom. Many people seem to leave their inhibitions at home when they travel. Why is that? One, you have more privacy away from home. If you want to make love before dinner, you know the phone's not going to ring. If you want to dress a little sexier when you usually do to go out to dinner, you won't run into somebody you know. You should also be more relaxed, as even a mini-vacation should be stress free. And you're not setting precedents. There can be a different set of rules that take over when traveling, so that just because you make love on the floor on a trip doesn't mean that you have to agree to it when you're back home.

There's no doubt that many people find that vacations are a romantic time and so the more vacation time you can have, the better will be your romance. And as to healing from the effects of empty-nest flu, well there's no better place to do it than away from home.

Sex Isn't Everything

But even I will admit that sex isn't everything and so you should also try to find other activities that you would enjoy doing together. To begin with, I might suggest something new, so that you're both at the same level of expertise. If a golfer convinced his spouse to take up golf or a bridge player lured her spouse into a game, it might be too frustrating for the experienced partner to wait until the spouse had caught on. But if you're both newbies, then you can enjoy learning

CONQUERING THE RAPIDS OF LIFE

some new skill together. And if you decide it's not for you and opt to drop this activity, neither one of you will be so invested that it will prove to be very disappointing.

Another suggestion is to make an effort to be with other people. Your children are gone and while they can never be replaced, sharing conversation with other adults would be a good substitute. So make a concerted effort to see other people, and not just the same people you see regularly, but some different people. Maybe a couple you only say hi to in church. Or some neighbors down the street that you just nod to in passing. Or the owner of some little shop that you stop in regularly. Some of these evenings may turn out to be boring, but if you do find some gems, then the overall effort will be worthwhile.

Charity Begins outside the Home

I would also like to suggest that if you're not already involved in your community, that you make an effort to get involved. By working at a soup kitchen, reading to kids stuck in a hospital, or registering people to vote, you'll not only be pursuing a worthwhile activity that will make you feel good, but you'll also be creating a store of new experiences that you can later discuss and share. Remember, one of your main goals is to put an end to boredom. So if the two of you can spend hours discussing the stories you've heard, trying to figure out ways to raise money for the group you're working for, and hopefully getting together with some of the new people you'll be meeting, you'll be gathering lots of firewood for keeping away the chills of boredom. That's why you'll find that by volunteering you'll pick up lots of positive energy that will inspire your relationship as well as your spirits.

Intellectual Pursuits

If you want to take your conversations into areas where they've never trod before, then the best path to follow is to take up some intellectual pursuits. There are many ways of pursuing this line of attack. One obvious avenue is to sign up for some classes. Most colleges offer classes that come under the rubric of continuing education, and since they do not count toward a degree, there are no impediments to enrolling, other than issues of finance and scheduling, and your grade is not what is important but how good a time you had. You can either both enroll in the same class or take separate subjects and then pass on some of the information you learned to each other.

A much simpler way of accomplishing the same end is through books. You could both read the same book and then discuss what you've read, or take different books on the same topic and compare notes.

I'm a big fan of museums, but it's not enough just to go and look at the art without really knowing what you are seeing. Check ahead to see if there's a particular exhibit planned for a nearby museum, and then go to the library and check out some books on the artist. Read up on the history of the artist and see what the critics have had to say, and then when you go to see the actual art you'll have a much broader perspective and find that the conversations you have will be a lot deeper than "That's nice" and "I like that one." I might even suggest that you choose artists that are a little more difficult. Some abstract painting makes no sense whatsoever to the casual observer, but perhaps by studying what the artist really had in mind, you'll gain a new appreciation for what all the fuss is about.

And if you want to have some competition thrown into your intellectual pursuits, bring in another couple, pick a topic to debate, and then study up to get ready for the big night. Just be careful to choose people who won't take it personally. And you might even switch sides in the middle so that no one has to spend an entire evening defending a position they don't really believe in.

What Not to Do with Other Couples

As a quick aside, I'm often asked about adding one or more other people into a couple's sex life. While I agree that a threesome or foursome would alleviate boredom in the bedroom, from my experience, it's also likely to destroy your relationship. Jealousy almost always rears its ugly head and the end result is just not worth it. So while I'm very much in favor of variety, when it comes to your sex life, fidelity is more important.

For Those Couples in a Damaged Relationship

As I said previously, some relationships are so badly damaged that when the children leave and remove the one basic reason to stay together, the marriage collapses, and whether or not the spouses continue to share the same roof, for all intents and purposes, they might as well be divorced. The sad truth is, there's not much to be done for those folks.

And then there are those teetering on the edge. They may not hate each other, but whatever love there was to start with has mostly dissipated. When the kids go and there's no good reason to stay together, they could go either way. If left to fate, probably the marriage would sink. If they work at it, however, the marriage does have a chance.

Seeking Help

I know that when you buy a self-help book you want information on how to help yourself through whatever problem
it is that you face. But I have to be honest here and tell you
that if you're in this particular predicament, your best bet is
not to try to handle this by yourself, but to go for professional counseling. That could mean a psychologist, a marital
counselor or therapist, or even a religious leader. There are
several reasons why a professional can help in a manner that
you just can't duplicate on your own that I want to go over
so as to convince you to go for help.

Many couples in this type of marriage fight a lot. They're
not necessarily fighting over anything in particular, but
they're angry that their lives are not the way they would like
and that anger comes out in all sorts of ways. So one vital
need that a counselor fulfills is that of referee. The situation
has to be defused before any progress can be made, and the
counselor can usually find ways of keeping the two combat-
ants apart. If not, then it probably means that the marriage
is too far gone to save.

Another role of a counselor is investigator. When a couple
comes to see me, the first thing I do is to talk to each one sep-
arately. I'll get two different stories, most of the time, and then
when I bring the two people together, I try to piece together
what is actually going on. Now it's not that the two people are
lying to me. After a while, people believe their own version of
the facts, whether they are true or not. But there are usually in-
consistencies and to bring them in line, one or both are going
to have to face the reality of the situation. That can be an important starting off point in arriving at a solution. And without
a counselor of some sort, that obstacle may never get breached.

And during these separate conversations, I sometimes
discover something else. Since I'm a sex therapist, it might be

a hidden affair, or an addiction to pornography, or a bad case of jealousy. Even if I don't raise this hidden issue with the other spouse, I can sometimes help the person deal with it so that at least it is no longer an obstacle to progress.

Something else a counselor can do is give "homework." Let's say that one of her complaints is that they never do anything fun. He's been saying he's too busy to go out, but maybe he actually just hasn't wanted to spend two hours with her discussing putting in a new kitchen, which he thinks is a frivolous expense, and which often leads to fights. What I'll tell them to do, for example, is to both read the paper that day, then go out for dinner and the only topics up for discussion were those that were reported in the newspaper. This will hopefully keep them from fighting. They both may actually enjoy the experience. That will make the odds that they'll go out for dinner again much more likely. And having given her an inducement, the pleasant evening, I may, then, be able to convince her to drop the idea of the kitchen since it's a constant source of irritation. If I'd told her not to talk about the kitchen in the first place, she would have thought I was picking on her and it wouldn't have worked. It was only by giving them both a homework assignment that I was able to show her the benefits of not talking about the kitchen. (I give other sorts of homework for those who come to me for sex therapy, but that's for another book.)

And, finally, a professional has training and years of experience to draw on. After a while you've just about seen it all, and you learn from this experience what advice works and what doesn't. That's the main difference between the advice of friends and family and a pro. They may think they know what you should do, but they could be wrong. Now a pro could be wrong too, but the odds that they're right are much higher since they've given this advice to others and received the feedback that it worked. Since each case is somewhat different, even a pro can make a mistake, but then they also have the wherewithal to correct that mistake, so you're definitely in better hands with professional guidance.

Case History: Teresa and Bill

Teresa knew she'd made a mistake marrying Bill a few months after the wedding. He was a dreamer, and she'd bought into those dreams not realizing that he was really too lazy to ever try to make them come true. She had children with him hoping that would push him into trying to get a better job, but he never changed. She turned out to be the main breadwinner, and even when he had long bouts of unemployment, she still had to take care of all the household duties. Once their children had left home, she knew that she had to get out of the marriage, but after twenty years, she wasn't sure how to do that, or whether she'd really be happier living alone. Teresa went to see a marital counselor, hoping that maybe there was something to be done to better her marriage. She told Bill she was going, but he refused to go with her. After about half a dozen visits, she came to the decision that she would ask for a separation from Bill.

There are many instances where one spouse is willing to go for therapy and the other isn't. While it's true that the therapist really needs to see both parties if he or she is going to be effective, if you're willing to go for help and your partner isn't, that's actually all the more reason why you should go, even by yourself.

Doing something active, like going to see a counselor, gives the message that you are serious. It tells your partner that this is not a situation that is going to solve itself, or that you're going to let slide. So by starting the ball rolling, so to speak, oftentimes you can get your partner to go along.

Of course, sometimes if your partner won't go for help it can mean that the situation is helpless. A therapist will help you to realize that, and then help you deal with the pain that is going to come from that realization. It's the avoidance of this pain that often keeps people from going for therapy. They realize that this step may be the first leading toward a separation. I know how difficult a decision this is, but in the long run, it's always the best decision. Staying in a relationship that brings daily doses of pain is just not a place where anyone should linger.

Some people get stuck on the issue of whether their relationship is at the point where professional intervention is needed. I say, if you can't make that decision, then the decision has been made for you; go to see a therapist who can help you to decide how bad things are and help you along to the next step. Don't be afraid that by walking into a therapist's office you're going to be stuck undergoing years of therapy. The type of counselors I'm suggesting you see usually work in a limited time frame. They're not looking to psychoanalyze you or your partner. They just want to help you start moving in the right direction, either toward a healthier relationship or a new one. In the long run, a professional will facilitate making the decision, so rather than agonize over this, the easy way out is actually to go to speak to somebody. My guess is that once you get your courage up and make an appointment, you'll immediately start to feel some relief.

What You Can Do

Hopefully I've convinced you to go for professional help, but if it's not in the cards, either because you live in the boonies where no help is available or for some other reason, let me say a few words about what you can do on your own.

If the two of you are fighting constantly, your first step has to be to diffuse this situation. The only way that you are going to make any improvements to your relationship is through better communication, and constant bickering is just not going to allow that to happen. The best thing you can do is to see if you can take certain issues off of the table. It could be sex, it could be finances, it could be your mother's weekly visits; whatever it is, agree not to talk about it. That doesn't mean you've stopped disagreeing on this issue, only that for the moment it's not up for discussion.

Another way to accomplish the same end is to agree to have a conversation on a certain topic. Look for subject matter that somehow won't bring you back to that bone of contention that you're trying to avoid. In other words, if finances are an issue, don't bring up a round-the-world cruise. But you could talk about ways of spending more time together.

If you're really stuck, use the written word to get yourselves started. It might be easier to say what you have to say in a note, especially if your partner tends toward being a hot head who reacts before even hearing what you have to say. Don't make it a long, drawn-out five-page letter. The objective is to work out a peace treaty so that you can start talking to each other, not settle every issue via a written agreement. Remember, the relationship between two married people is supposed to be based on love, not logic. I'm assuming you did once love each other very much, and it is only by reconnecting directly with each other that you can light love's fires once again.

If sex has been a sore spot, then that might be the main issue to take out of play. The ground rules have to say, we're going to talk because we want to get to know each other once again. This particular occasion, or the next few, can't lead to sex. Removing sexual tension can actually make things easier. When sex is in the air, it complicates everything, but if you both agree that these conversations are not part of foreplay, you might actually make some progress.

In addition to removing certain subjects, it's also a good idea to have some defined goals. It could be as simple as going out to the movies together. Seeing a movie gives you something to do and something to talk about that shouldn't lead to controversy. Another advantage of going out to see a movie is that it gets you out of the house. As I mentioned before, leaving the homestead creates subtle changes that can reduce tension and lead to improvements in your relationship. Then, hopefully out of that one movie, you can graduate to having a movie night.

As you can see, the idea is to take small, baby steps. You can't repair years and years of damage in one fell swoop. You have to have realistic goals that can be met. If you can begin to turn things around and establish a momentum, then you might be able to speed up the process. But it's always better to take it slow as there's much less of a chance of making some misstep that will set you back.

Keep Your Individuality

And when trying to piece back together a relationship, always keep in mind that you are two individuals and you can't sew yourselves together to become Siamese twins. As I've been saying through the kayak metaphor, you do need some space. Perhaps because the kids are now gone, you'll be freer to give each other some room to maneuver. When you're worrying about kids, you don't want to also have to worry about too much else. For example, if one of you wanted to leave the rat race and start a one-man business, that's something that you might not be able to do when there are kids at home. It might mean working long days and nights, as well as the risk of financial failure. But once the kids are gone (and college payments are not so much an issue) then you can afford to give your spouse that kind freedom. You're attached, but it's a voluntary attachment, and not one kept together out of necessity. And those types of attachments are often the strongest.

When Operation Repair Breaks Down

Just because you are running "operation repair" doesn't mean it's going to work. There's a good chance that after much effort you're going to find that the two of you really are no longer compatible. At that point, don't go into denial. If your relationship has run its course, then you have to learn to accept that fact. It's harder to do it on your own, but many people do it, and if that's the only way of handling it, then that's what you have to do. The result will mean an even emptier nest, maybe even a new, smaller one, but as time elapses, you will heal and recover, and when you look back you'll accept that it was the best course of action, under the circumstances.

CHAPTER 7

Psychological Boulders

THERE ARE MANY DANGERS WHEN PADDLING through rapids, the most visible being the various rocks and boulders that can suddenly rise up in your path that you have to paddle around or go crashing into. I've gone over the issues of health that these rocks might represent, and now I want to deal with some of the psychological dangers of the Whitewater Years, beyond empty-nest syndrome, which I've just covered.

One reason that people stumble over a variety of psychological issues at this stage of their lives is that this is a time when they find themselves thinking about a reassessment. Why this sudden urge to examine what they've accomplished to date? Maybe it's because of the fear of looking too far forward and having to contemplate what their old age will be like that sends them looking backward to see where they stand vis-à-vis their original goals. Or maybe it's because they've reached quite a few of the goals they'd originally set for themselves—like getting married, raising children, and carving out a reasonably successful career—that they start looking around for new ones. Recent surveys have shown that 50 percent of people are not happy at their jobs, and that percentage is even higher for baby boomers, so it could be this dissatisfaction that drives them toward searching out the reasons they feel the way they do. Others in this age bracket are forced to reassess because their companies have decided that the premium they are being paid for their years of experience is no longer worth it, and the decision has been made to replace them with someone younger who will work for much less. For some, this is a case of reading the writing on the wall, while others discover what management thinks of the gray hair they've accumulated on the job only when they get their pink slips.

Another group of "Whitewaterites" found the events of September 11, 2001, an inducement to get them thinking about making changes. It made them realize that their lives could be cut short at any moment and that if they wanted to fill their days with the most satisfaction possible, it might mean trying something new.

And, of course, people never lived as long as we do in the twenty-first century. If you started this particular career path when you got out of college, even if you changed your place of employment several times, you've been pursuing the same type of job for thirty years or more. And conceivably you have another twenty years of work ahead of you. Being a (fill in the blank) for fifty years is going to take its toll, no matter how much you enjoyed this line of work when you started.

So as you can see, there are plenty of reasons why more and more people in their fifties are taking a careful look at where they are at this point in their lives and whether or not they'd like to be heading in another direction.

A Common Mistake to Avoid

Case History: Eileen

Eileen was an attorney. At age fifty-two she should have been a partner in a firm long ago, but she could never stay in one place long enough to make partner. There was always some factor that she couldn't stand—a boss, a secretary, a client—and so she would move on to a new place. She had tried making it on her own, but she hated the pressure of having to bring in new clients. Currently she works for an insurance company, defending them against claims, but she absolutely hates her job and probably won't last very long. In fact, she's rethinking the whole idea of being a lawyer and is thinking of going back to school to become a social worker.

Self-examination is always a good idea. If you're dashing through life at a helter-skelter pace, never having any time to think whether or not you're on the right path, then it wouldn't be surprising if you wound up someplace where you'd rather not be. The only way to avoid such an outcome is to put aside some time to reflect on your life, and then make the necessary adjustments.

However, I want to caution you against making one common mistake, which is to automatically assume that any dissatisfaction you might feel is the result of your job. Yes, you spend eight or more hours a day at work, and you might be unhappy for much of that time, but it might not be the actual workplace that is at fault. An equally important factor for how you feel is who you are. If you're dissatisfied with your present job, you might also have felt dissatisfied with any job if, instead of your line of work, it was something else in your life that was causing you to be dissatisfied. So don't be so quick to change careers until you are certain of the cause of your feelings. Remember, there are people with great careers who are miserable and others who have to toil at some job that doesn't pay much or give them much satisfaction and yet are very happy with their lives overall.

If the answer to your dissatisfaction lies elsewhere, you had better find that out before you give up one career to start another. Let's say that what you need is an outlet for your creative juices. True, your current job may not be the place to fulfill that urge, but then again, neither might any other job. Maybe your artistic bent would only be satisfied by painting. Since it's highly unlikely you could earn a living as a painter, unless you wanted to paint houses, that's a creative activity that you would need to do on your own time. It might take a concerted effort on your part to find the time to paint (or sculpt or write or learn how to play a musical instrument), but at least you would be heading in the right direction rather than changing jobs and winding up frustrated once again.

You Don't Need to Decide by Yourself

You're the only person who can tell if you feel dissatisfied and in need of a change, but that doesn't necessarily mean that you're also the best person to decide what that change should be. I've said before not to shy away from using someone else's expertise when faced with a problem, and this is another instance when you might want to look to professional guidance.

Perhaps by seeking out a career advisor who can give you a battery of personality tests, you'll be able to discover why you're feeling the need to change and what type of work or activity would give you the most satisfaction. Or by talking to your religious leader, you might discover that doing some outside charity work would give more meaning to your life than a new job (and that you could more easily get the free time on your present job than in one you were contemplating). And if you're thinking about heading into an entirely new career, go through your list of contacts and see who you might know in any of the fields you are considering. It's better to find out ahead of time from someone experienced in that area what the potential pitfalls are than to have to discover them yourself after a long and complicated career change.

At the very least, I would suggest heading for your public library or neighborhood bookstore to seek out some books on this topic. I made quite a career change in my fifties but still, this isn't my area of expertise. But by reading up on the subject, you might find some concepts that will prove very useful to you.

Listen to the Knocking

But there is one tip that I would like to offer that is based on my experience. Opportunity does come knocking from time to time, so even if you're not looking for a change, don't dismiss that knocking out of hand. If an offer comes your way, consider it carefully. Change is scary, and if you like the people you work with and don't mind your job, the easy path might be to stay put. But we all need challenges in life in order to reach our highest potential. So if a job offer has the potential to raise the bar for you, it's something you should consider. Always taking the easy way out rarely gets you very far in life.

Self-Assessing for Two

So far I've been addressing these issues as if their only impact was on your life alone. But if you're part of a couple, any changes that you go through will definitely affect your relationship, and the same is true for any changes your spouse might try. I would think that you know enough to discuss a change as significant as looking for a different career with your spouse. But there are some men who won't have job-related discussions with their wives because their manhood is very much tied to their job, and so they keep everything related to their work life to themselves. Some men will even hide from their wives the fact that they've lost a job. Such behavior is obviously counterproductive when it comes to having a good relationship. But even assuming that you do tell your spouse what you are contemplating, the question remains, how much should your partner's input count? Does he or she hold veto power or does he or she only have an advisory position?

Clearly the answer depends, to some degree, on how much your spouse will be affected. For example, if you would like to switch jobs to one that will have more meaning for you but will cut your income in half, then your partner in life certainly should have a say in all of this. You might also find, when bringing up this subject, that your spouse was having similar feelings. It would complicate matters dramatically if you were both to switch jobs at the same time, so just deciding on the batting order would be an important first step.

It's certainly better to have such discussions before a crisis is reached. So even if you've only been thinking about this in a casual sort of way, share your feelings with your spouse. There will be much less pressure if you can have such discussions when there are many options than if you're staring a forced career move in the face. And if there's anyone who knows you, it should be your spouse, so the advice that he or she offers will be valuable.

And what if you're on the other side of this issue, and it is your spouse who has come to you to talk about his or her thoughts on a new career? The most important thing your spouse is looking for is your support. Changing careers is unnerving, to say the least, and it's important to know that the other areas of his or her life are going to remain stable as the process runs its course. So by telling him or her that you'll be there offering as much support as you can will take a big load off of his or her mind.

Career Change Concerns

The major concerns about a change of employment are often about financial issues. The odds are that at the beginning of this process the family finances are going to suffer. You can't expect to make as much money at a job that you have little experience in as one where you're an old pro. That's going to mean adjusting your standard of living. If you're both not willing to cut down on expenses, then it's going to be difficult to pull this maneuver off successfully. This is especially true if the new direction requires additional education. Going for a degree in another area, for example, can take years. That's going to require sacrifices all around so everyone has to be in agreement before you forge ahead.

But there is a long list of other concerns that have to be dealt with as well. If this change is going to require a significant increase in work hours (such as would occur if one spouse enrolled in night school and spent the weekends studying), the other partner is going to be left alone more. If this was already an issue, he or she may not be willing to give up even more time as a couple. Or a new career might mean moving. That certainly is an issue both partners must agree on. There may be questions of pensions and benefits. What if this new career involves opening a home office; how would the other person take to that concept?

Discussions on these types of topics can bring out different reactions. If the relationship is not on solid ground, it could make things even more shaky. Asking a spouse to make additional compromises could be the straw that breaks the camel's back. So you have to be delicate when handling these topics, and as I said earlier, the earlier in the process you begin, so that it's not as if you are presenting them with a fait accompli, the better the results you'll have.

To Retire or Not to Retire

Let me say to you right now, I have no intention of retiring. My attorney once gave me some knitting needles saying if I got tired of being Dr. Ruth I could always sit in a rocking chair and knit, and I have no intention of ever taking up that offer. Now that's not to say retirement isn't right for some people. Especially people whose jobs require a lot of physical labor, which would become impossible to do after a certain age. All I have to do is move my lips, which doesn't take that much effort.

But while I agree that people in some fields need to stop what they're doing after a time, I'm still not sure they should spend the rest of their days sitting by a pool in Florida or Arizona. If you want your mind to stay sharp, you have to use it, and vegetating isn't going to provide much exercise for your brain. However, just because one is over sixty-five and still working doesn't mean that you have to be doing the same job you always did. Many people who are over sixty-five and still work end up switching to some other type of employment, one that requires fewer hours or less physical activity.

But wait a minute, you're saying, I'm not in that age group yet. I've got ten or more years before I turn sixty-five. That may be true, but my aim is to prepare you psychologically for when you get there. If all you can think about is the day you turn sixty-five and can start a never-ending series of golf games, and then when those golf matches get postponed for five or ten years, you're going to be sorely disappointed. So it's better to prepare psychologically for the real world. And the odds are that you will be working past the age of sixty-five.

One reason for this has to do with demographics. If you're in your fifties, then you're part of the baby boom generation. But the next generation is considerably smaller in size. So the American economy is going to need workers, and

a natural pool are those who in earlier years would have re-
tired. So even if you didn't really want to keep working, the
business world is going to do its best to lure you to stay.

Another reason that people keep working is financial.
Americans have been saving less and less, and so many people are financially ill-prepared to retire, especially as Social
Security is not as rock solid as it once was. Another financial
consideration is health care costs. Older people have rising
health care costs, and those costs have only been heading up
and up. In fact, many older people who work these days do
so mostly for the health care benefits.

So for argument's sake, let's say that you are going to
keep working beyond your sixty-fifth birthday. The odds are
that you are not going to be holding the same job you've got
now. Your employer is not going to want to continue to give
you raises every year for the next twenty years. So you'll
probably wind up someplace else. And the time to start planning for where that will be is now.

For example, let's say that you don't have to use com-
puters in your current position. It would be a good idea to
begin learning now so that if this next job requires that skill,
you'll be able to check yes on the proper forms. Or maybe
you'd enjoy teaching, but don't have any education credits.
Well, then, you should enroll in a college and take some
courses at night. Or perhaps you'd want to start your own
business. That might require putting aside some extra
money. In other words, if you'll have to change careers, and
that change will require some preparation, you'd better start
getting yourself ready.

Now, of course, this is an issue that you must discuss
with your spouse. If one of you has these visions of a life of
leisure and the other intends to work until he or she drops,
someone is going to have a very long face, and maybe for
many, many years. Maybe the compromise you reach is to

move to a warmer climate, but someplace that also offers the possibility for employment. But if that's the case, then you might want to start researching where that place might be ahead of time.

By the way, you should look at any planning you do as a fun activity, and not a chore. If you can get excited about what the future holds for you, even if it is not spending your days on the beach, that would be an important step. Having a positive attitude often creates a positive outcome, so this planning offers additional benefits.

While it's important to plan ahead, you also have to be realistic. As you get older, getting up to go to work will be a bit tougher and other circumstances might change that will put a crimp in your plans. So inject a bit of realism into your dreams so that you don't start thinking that this new career will turn you into the next Bill Gates.

The Sandwich Generation

One of the ways that your plans may be forced to change is if you find yourself caring for older parents. I touched on the subject of the sandwich generation earlier, but it requires a bit more examination. I say a bit, but one could actually write an entire book on the subject. Being in prime sandwich generation territory can toss you around as if you were in rapids, after you've fallen out of your kayak!

The sandwich generation refers to those people who still are responsible for their children, even if that "only" means paying for their college expenses (though with so many more grownup children moving back home, it could mean actually having them under your roof full time), and who also have had to assume some or all of the responsibilities for one or more parents, almost always due to their failing health.

I'm going to start by telling you that I lost all of my family in the Holocaust. I never had the opportunity of caring for my aging parents. I used the word *opportunity* on purpose, because if your parents are old, then that means you had them through all the good times—the births, the graduations, and so forth. They probably babysat for their grandchildren, cooked for them, spoiled them. So, yes, they may be a burden at the end of their days, but you must look at this with the proper perspective.

Looking at it that way doesn't make it any easier. Nor does it mean that you won't miss fulfilling those dreams you had for foreign travel and turning the guest room into a study. But you'll need some sort of anchor to hang on to, and the past joys will make as good a one as any. That's particularly true in cases where the older person is suffering from some form of dementia, as people who have been sweet their entire lives may become vicious and nasty.

If the two of you are forced to care for one or more elderly parent, it is vital to your relationship that you do it together. It doesn't matter whose parent it is. That's not totally true, of course. The person whose parent it is will have more of a guilty conscience and will do more. That's only natural. But you should try to act as much as a team as possible. Remember, just because it's the husband's mother, it could just as well be the wife's. This is a duty that you accepted when you got married and now your parents/in-laws are calling in their chips. You have to respond as positively as possible because one day you might be in the same boat and you want to set the right example for your kids so that they don't wash their hands of you.

Traditionally, doctors were men and nurses were women. Luckily that's changing so that there are many more women doctors and male nurses. Why am I bringing this up? Because there's a good chance that an elderly parent is going to

CONQUERING THE RAPIDS OF LIFE

CONQUERING THE RAPIDS OF LIFE

CONQUERING THE RAPIDS OF LIFE

CONQUERING THE RAPIDS OF LIFE

CONQUERING THE RAPIDS OF LIFE

CONQUERING THE RAPIDS OF LIFE

CONQUERING THE RAPIDS OF LIFE

CONQUERING THE RAPIDS OF LIFE

need some nursing, and the burden shouldn't fall entirely on the wife. "You don't expect me to help my mother get out of the bathtub" I can hear you men saying. Please, let's drop the Victorian prudery. She changed your diapers when you were small, and if you have to help her out now, then that's what you have to do, even if she's dripping wet and naked. For the most part I think this false modesty is an excuse to avoid having to do your fair share. But even if it's not, you just have to get over it. If one-half of a couple is doing all the work tending the elderly person, that person is going to resent it and that's going to have a serious impact on your relationship. If you can share the burden, at least the stress won't fall so heavily on one person and that will make it more bearable. And if you have children at home, then they have to help out as well. They'll complain but it will be a good lesson; one that you might benefit from twenty years or so from now.

Learning to Adjust

And there's one more thing having your ailing parents around will do to you; it will make you think of your own future as an elderly person. It's much harder to deny that old age is around the corner when you're faced with an older parent every minute of the day. So the question is, how do you adjust to all of this? How do you maintain your sanity?

If nothing else, the Whitewater Years are a time to make adjustments. You'll be adjusting to your changing health and your changing lifestyle. Certainly having to deal with aging parents is going to take adjusting to. But while your life is acting like a roller coaster, it's also the period when you've managed to become set in your ways. You may feel that you're entitled to a little routine, that you've earned it, and here you are faced with all this turbulence. That's going to cause what's known as *cognitive dissonance*. In other words, the reality you are facing is different from what you expected and that is upsetting.

If you really are having a hard time dealing with this, then go for professional help. But if at least a shoulder to cry on would be of great assistance, then turn to your spouse. What you might have to do is to alternate being strong and weak. It's hard to be strong every day. You need to relax once in a while. Your partner has to learn to read the signs so that he or she knows when you're at the edge of your limits and can take over. You may be exchanging roles for quite some time, years in fact, and like it or not, you're going to have to learn to be flexible, even if that has never been your strong point.

This is a lesson that people who undergo calamities are forced to learn. If a tornado or hurricane or earthquake has turned your life upside down, then what choice do you have but to learn to walk on the ceiling? But during the Whitewater Years, things appear relatively normal from the outside. The pressures don't seem all that bad, and yet they can be considerable. And believe it or not, that can actually make it harder on you. You want to keep up appearances. You want to maintain the illusion to those around you that everything is going swimmingly, when in fact you're drowning.

When a young couple has a small baby, everyone knows how difficult that can be and so friends, neighbors, and relatives all chip in to help. That doesn't usually happen when the one who needs caring is an elderly person. But it should. As a society we are going to have to use a little creativity to figure out how to cope with the increasing number of our citizens who are, by any definition, really old. When you look at the statistics, the number of people who are going to be older than one hundred in a decade or so are just amazing. So while we'll still need babysitters, we're also going to need "nanasitters." We're going to have to figure out a way to relieve those people in the sandwich generation of having to shoulder the entire burden of caring for an older parent. I know that there are visiting nurses and home care aides, but they can be costly and difficult to find in smaller cities and suburbs.

One immediate suggestion I can make is to find some neighbors who are in the same situation you're in and offer to help each other out. Or as a community, you might want to create a version of day care for the elderly residents in the neighborhood. I know there are senior centers, but those are usually for those who can take care of themselves. I'm suggesting a place where those who need help can be taken for a few hours.

And you're also going to have to find a way to integrate your siblings into the equation. Maybe your house is the only one with a spare bedroom, but then your brothers and sisters have to do something to make up for your taking on this extra burden. You should make a fairly iron-clad contract about this, if possible, when you first agree to it, otherwise there could be some "misunderstandings" down the line. For example, perhaps a sibling might have to give up a week's vacation to stay at your house so that you and your spouse can get away. That would only be fair because you'd be giving up so much of your free time on a daily basis. An alternative is to have them kick in to pay for a caregiver so that you can take a break. Agreements like these will be easier to work out ahead of time than to ask for once a parent has moved in with you. This type of situation is a heavy burden, and likely to get worse than better as an elderly person becomes more and more frail. So don't take it lightly and try to get the most help that you can at the very beginning.

Feeling Guilty

As good-hearted as you may be, it's easy to feel frustrated in a situation such as this. You had a plan for the empty-nest years, at least one of sorts, and now it's been turned upside down. And since the only solution is for the elderly parent to pass away or become so sick that a nursing home is required, every time you say to yourself, "When is this going to end?" you're going to feel guilty.

It's natural to feel frustrated by a situation like this. You can't stop yourself and you shouldn't punish yourself for these thoughts. After all, that's all they are, thoughts. You weren't seriously planning on doing the old person in. I've used the word *frustration*, which I think is correct, but your body is going to react as if you were angry or scared. In other words, when you're feeling very frustrated, your level of adrenaline is going to go higher just the way it would if you were a caveman facing a dangerous animal, the so-called fight or flight syndrome. This chemical reaction is not one that you can control. You can tell yourself to calm down, but that won't necessarily help. But notice that the opposite component of fight is flight. In other words, to dissipate your anger, the best thing you can do is something active, like running, if you're up for that, or even a fast walk around the block. If you can't leave the house because the person in your care needs constant watching, then jog in place for a bit. Or put on a record and dance. Or get a step stool and climb up and down twenty times. Anything to use up that adrenaline in a physical way instead of letting it drive you mentally crazy.

And if exercise alone won't calm you down, then go to your doctor and see what other types of help might be appropriate. It's not that I'm very much in favor of taking tranquilizers and the like, but sometimes they are necessary, at least for a short period of time.

Maintain Your Intimacy

I would also suggest that you don't let the presence of this elderly person ruin your sex life. It's one thing to pretend to youngsters that their parents don't have sex, and so wait until they are in bed or whatever. But you don't have to be as protective of a parent, who, after all, had a sex life, whether or not you, as their child, want to admit it. And this is an area where I think you need to establish some guidelines early on. In other words, if you allow the presence of this person to inhibit you in the first week, then it's going to be hard to overcome that as time goes by. But if at least one of you grabs the bull by the horns, so to speak, and pushes your sex life up a notch or two so as to set the bar as high as possible, then even if you do have some off weeks where sex is on the back burner, it won't be so hard to raise the level back up again.

Learning to Look Ahead

When you were a child, you couldn't wait for your next birthday. That anticipation lasted until you were twenty-one and could be considered an adult in every aspect. After that, birthdays were less anticipated, and probably by the time you reached thirty, they were something you were beginning to want to avoid. Certainly many people in their Whitewater Years would prefer to skip birthday celebrations altogether, but more important than that 1 day a year is your attitude the other 364 days.

Case History: Fred

When Fred looked back at his life, he felt a lot of contentment. He was fifty-five and he had earned a degree from a college he still felt a lot of attachment to, loved the woman he married, adored his children, and was financially secure. But when he looked ahead, he felt nothing but dread. Fred had always been goal oriented. It seemed that he'd already reached all the goals he'd set for himself. Without anything to shoot for, he wasn't sure what his purpose in life was, and he often had trouble getting out of bed in the morning after a lifetime where he hadn't been able to wait for the alarm to ring.

Fred's negative outlook is more common in men than in women. Studies have shown that women in their Whitewater Years report higher levels of personal growth and positive relationships with others than men do. If a man has invested himself mostly in his job and then realizes that he's reached a pinnacle in that arena, it's not surprising that he might find himself at a loss. But, of course, there are many women who wind up feeling the same way, particularly if they invested most of themselves into raising their children and those children are now grown adults and in no need of her ministrations.

The trick to solving this delemma is, once again, preparation. If you follow one narrow track, it makes sense that you might feel lost when you were approaching the end of it. But if you had lots of different interests, then your major dilemma will be deciding which one to choose next. If you've not broadened your scope, in terms of activities, friends, interests, then don't delay. I don't want to say the Whitewater Years are your last opportunity to broaden your outlook, because I think it's never too late to begin a new path, but what the Whitewater Years offer you is a chance to make some mistakes. Let's say you try to take up painting and six months later you're still drawing stick figures. It won't be a major psychological blow because it was just a hobby, after all. But if you'd planned to take up painting on your retirement and at that time had shown no aptitude, then you would feel badly and might have a harder time finding a new direction to take. So don't paint yourself into a corner; use your Whitewater Years to look around you and find new directions.

The Grim Reaper

I touched on the subject of death, but it's one that deserves some more thought. In the Whitewater Years, death becomes more of a player than it was before. Now it won't just be older relatives who will die, but more and more contemporaries. And as sad as attending those funerals can be, they also bring with them a new component—fear—because now you have to begin to accept the possibility of your own death. In fact, you have to start planning for it. You must have wills, if you haven't already made them. And you should start thinking about estate planning. This is so far from my area of expertise that I'm not going to touch those subjects, but there are definitely psychological components to the creation of all these documents.

There's never an easy time to deal with death. I certainly wasn't prepared for it when I was ten and lost my entire family. But it is a little bit easier to handle when you have a spouse who can comfort you. If the person who died was closer to one of you, the other has to shoulder more of the load to make the situation as bearable as possible. In addition to literally offering a shoulder to cry on, you have to step in and handle responsibilities that the other would normally do so that they can deal with their grief. And to some extent, you have to encourage that grief. There is a mourning period that we all have to go through at the death of someone close, and it's during that time that you should allow your emotions to take over. Then you'll have an easier time dealing with the death and will be able to substitute good memories for the bad ones that occurred right at the time of death. But if you bottle up all of your emotions, trying to avoid the pain of the grief, then you also block the good thoughts about the person who passed away, and so you never fully recover.

Your role as a significant other is to facilitate the mourning process. Encourage your partner to cry and be sad for a time. And then help them to remember the deceased in the best possible light. Find pictures that will stir up happy memories. Remind them of funny or moving incidents. Invite other friends or relatives over to share in these moments. Do as good a job as you can for them, and then they'll be there to help you out when the need arises.

CHAPTER 8

Rekindling Your Romance

YOU MIGHT THINK THAT AFTER HAVING LIVED together for such a long time, especially while you were on that comfy raft peacefully sailing down the river of life, that the state of your romance would be in excellent shape. While I certainly hope that's the case, it's not true for many couples. The main reason is that their raft was a crowded and busy place. Romance blooms best when a couple has some time to relax and enough peace and quiet that they can concentrate on each other, at least once in a while. With a busy schedule and kids constantly interrupting, romance often gets pushed aside. That's not to say that sex can't and won't occur under less than ideal conditions, but it's often not as passionate as when a couple has the time and attention to fully devote to each other. And while rushed sex may be better than no sex, as soon as the opportunity for improving your love life pokes its head up, you should grab it.

So in terms of your romance, is there any advantage to being in two separate kayaks fighting the rapids rather than on that raft? Believe it or not, I think there is. For a long time I've said that skiers make the best lovers. I've targeted skiers because I'm partial to them, as I love to ski, but the logic that

I use can apply to any active person, including those who love to shoot whitewater rapids. If you've spent the day skiing, you're going to be exhilarated after your last run. Your legs may be a little tired, but your spirits will be soaring. You'll relive those great runs you had and you'll be feeling more alive than ever. When two people are sharing that skiers' high, they're in the perfect mood to have fabulous sex. Their passions are running wild and they can't wait to share a nice hot tub and wrap their bodies around each other.

Now skiers don't necessarily go down the slopes together. One half of the couple might be more advanced than the other, or prefer a slope with more moguls. It's certainly not a sport where you can spend time holding hands. And, the same is true of kayakers or rock climbers or mountain bike riders or long-distance runners. But when you're done with any of these vigorous activities, your cheeks are all red, your blood is circulating at top speed, and you feel on top of the world. Compare that to two people who have sat in front of the television for umpteen hours. They may have been side by side, but they feel lethargic, perhaps bloated from the snacks they ate, and with their blood circulating at a snail's pace, they're certainly not in peak form to have sex.

Now I realize that these kayaks that I mention are metaphoric, but whether you're actually doing something physical or just leading a life that is rich with many interesting pursuits, that's going to create an environment that is perfectly suited to romance and sex. So you could get that feeling of exhilaration after having written some verses of poetry that you really liked, or purchased the stamp you'd been looking for to fill your collection, or digging up all the weeds in your rose garden, or baking a batch of your partner's favorite cookies, or even finishing a tough crossword puzzle. Yes, I think it's better if what you do has a physically active component, but it's really your brain that is your primary sex organ, and so whatever you do that makes your brain active and alive is what will help to set off sparks between the two of you.

Case History: Becky and Marvin

Becky and Marvin had been married for twenty-five years, and they would probably stay married until they died, though neither one loved the other. Becky was very religious, and since her religion forbids divorce, she felt she had to stick it out. Marvin wasn't the type of guy who would want to fix his own dinner or do laundry, so he was satisfied having a live-in maid. In between long bouts of silence were fights of epic proportions. When they were apart, they never stopped complaining about each other to friends and relatives, and they hadn't slept in the same bed for ten years, though from time to time Becky allowed Marvin to have sex with her, though she never had an orgasm from these couplings. To her, sex was just part of her wifely duties. Theirs was a marriage of inconvenience, and yet the underlying structure made it as hardy as any marriage could be.

A Good Relationship Is Vital

Since I admit that you can have an okay sex life even if your marriage isn't all that it should be, perhaps some of you are saying, "Well, as long as we can have sex, it's not that important if our relationship is that great." This is a delusion that you should rid yourself of as soon as possible. First of all, as I just said, your sex life will be a lot better if your relationship is operating on all pistons. But there's a lot more to a marriage than just sex. In fact, recent studies have shown that a good marriage can actually add years to your life, while a bad one can take years off.

This set of statistics has been labeled the marriage benefit. It shows two trends. The first is that married couples live longer than people who are single, divorced, or widowed. Married people generally have fewer illnesses, and it's been shown that middle-age men, who are unmarried, in Western countries at least, are twice as likely to die than their married counterparts. (In the short run, as obviously we all will die at some point.)

But it turns out that this benefit seems only to apply to good marriages. If the marriage is going badly, then the medical benefits disappear and turn negative and are much more negative for wives stuck in bad marriages. If there is a lot of tension in a marriage, that leads to depression, a mental state more often encountered by women, and that has a definite negative impact on a person's health. For example, one study showed that people in bad marriages recovering from heart attacks were 1.8 times as likely to die within the next four years as those in good marriages. While that statistic might not surprise you so much, another study showed that people in low-quality marriages even have more cavities and incidences of gum disease! That one sure surprised me, but I guess it all has to do with your body's ability to fight against any sort of illness, and if your spirits are low, that will have a negative effect on your immune system.

So I want you to look at the information I'm giving you in this chapter not as frivolous but rather as vital to your good health. And remember, a relationship can rarely stay in a steady state. Either it's going uphill or downhill. The incline might be slight, but over the course of many years, the result can be severe.

Admittedly, you may have been distracted regarding the condition of your marriage when the kids were around, but that's probably not the case in your Whitewater Years. And this sudden attention might exaggerate your reaction to any negativity. For example, you may have a "junk" room in your house that you rarely go into, and when you do, because there's only one light bulb and the shades are drawn, you never look at it all that carefully. Then, one day you decide to straighten it up, maybe even with the aim of making it into a sewing room or a study. You go inside, raise the shades, and you're astounded at how bad it is. Never having paid much attention to the state this room was in, it hadn't bothered you. But now, looking at it carefully, you're disgusted.

That junk room could be the state of your marriage. If you were too busy to undergo much of a self-examination, then you didn't realize how bad things had gotten. But now, when you look closely at it, you can't help but notice the disrepair. So if yours is a marriage that will have a negative impact on your health, don't delay in giving it the spring cleaning it needs.

Raising the Heat

A relationship could be compared to a fire. It may take a while for the wood to catch, but when it does, boy do those flames roar. And as long as you keep adding wood, the fire will go on and on. But if you neglect it, the fire will die out. If there's no heat left whatsoever, it's going to take quite an effort to get that fire going again. It will be worse than starting off from scratch because all the old burned wood, now ashes, will have to be cleaned away first. But if there are even a few hot embers left, then it will be a lot easier. You can add some small sticks, blow hard at the embers for a while, and hopefully you'll have a decent fire that can grow to as large a blaze as it once was.

So how do you translate this metaphor into the reality of your relationship? I'm going to assume that there are at least a few embers, and hopefully even some flames, still flickering. If the fire has totally died out, you're probably going to need the help of a marriage counselor. But if it's just in a weakened state, then you can definitely get it going again on your own.

Of course you need the desire to make this happen. So the first step is to tell yourself that you want to make some major improvements to your relationship. As they say, where there's a will there's a way, but if you are not interested, then it's just not going to happen.

What if you have some doubts? What if you start thinking, "I've been with this person for twenty or thirty years, I've heard all her/his funny stories, I know his/her body too well, maybe it's time for a change?" That's a fair question. You shouldn't want to jumpstart this relationship just because it's there. You should take a good look at it. And at yourself.

No relationship is perfect. If you were to go out and find someone else, I'll admit the flames would burn higher for a time without much effort. But three months later, you could find yourself worse off. And it could take you years to find this new flame, and there's even the possibility that you would never find anyone else. I'm not saying that you should stay in a relationship just because you might wind up spending the rest of your days alone, but that risk should be part of the overall equation.

On the other hand, if you look at your current relationship I'm sure you can think of lots of good reasons to stay together. You have a family, especially children and maybe even grandchildren, that would be seriously impacted if you were to split. You've got decades worth of memories that only your partner can really appreciate sharing with you. You've got a well-established comfort level that allows you to act much more freely than you could with anyone else. You've got shared friends, shared belongings, shared tastes, and, most importantly, shared emotions. At one time you were very much in love. That means a lot because it proves that you were compatible and the likelihood is that, under the right, romantic conditions, you can restore any parts of that love that have since faded. Of course, if the relationship has soured, all this history may not be worth all that much, but if you're still compatible, then it's worth quite a lot.

There's that old axiom about the greener grass on the other side of the fence being an illusion, and old as it is, it still has a lot of merit. While there's always the chance that you could improve your love life scanning those greener pastures, the odds favor your doing better with the spouse you already have than with somebody new. The trick is to work on that relationship so that it's in the best shape it can be, and I believe you'll find the rewards well worth the effort.

Creating a Relationship Shape-Up Plan

I've said before that the biggest danger to a relationship is boredom, so part one of your relationship shape-up plan should be to find areas where boredom has been allowed to take over, and then doing something about it. Here are some suggestions:

- Instead of giving each other a peck on the cheek when you leave in the morning, set aside sixty seconds to indulge in a real kiss.
- Raid each other's closets and drawers and wear something unexpected around the house.
- Make love in the kitchen.
- Prepare a macrobiotic dinner or have lobster for breakfast.
- To spice up dinnertime, read *Lady Chatterley's Lover* out loud.

- Learn a new word every day and make a point of using it in conversation.
- Have a sack race around the living room.

Do some of these suggestions seem silly? Maybe they are, but so what? The idea isn't to become instant geniuses and have stirring intellectual conversations about the origins of the universe. Oh, that would be a great suggestion too, if you could do it, but I don't want to make it seem so complicated that you give up without even trying. To get your personal battle against boredom started, you just have to do anything that pops into your head that is unexpected.

And here's my most important suggestion: don't say no. If your spouse suggests something a little outrageous or silly or inane, go with the flow. If it doesn't work out, then you never have to do it again. And don't take such a serious attitude about all of this. Laugh instead of getting angry. You have to be willing to experiment if you're not going to be boring. If you always play it safe, then you'll only do what's expected, and that's . . . boring.

But boredom isn't the only danger to a marriage. Lack of communication is another very serious challenge to maintaining a good relationship. For the two of you to fully connect when you are together, you must give all your attention to your partner. You have to concentrate on your partner's words, expressions, and body language so that you can respond appropriately. Love and romance are about sharing and giving, even though the feelings that result, particularly orgasms, are something that only you can feel. If you can learn to connect to your partner when you're both feeling highly charged, then that connection can be intense, on a physical level but also emotionally and intellectually.

Making Use of Your New Status

The major opportunity that the Whitewater Years have to offer to your relationship is the means to avoid distractions. If you want to unplug the phone and have a candlelight dinner, there's nothing to stop you (even if the food is takeout). If you're both working, it might not be something you can do every night. But you can certainly plan on doing it once or twice a week, even if it means having dinner at 10 P.M. In other words you can make the state of your romance a top priority in many different ways than you could before.

Reconnecting

During those twenty-odd years when you had the care of children on your mind, you were likely to let your partner fend for him- or herself a bit. But now, if you're going to make a sacrifice, you can do it for your partner. And in the long run, those sacrifices will be very much appreciated and can do a lot for your relationship. Here are some examples:

- One partner likes to "putter" in the garden. The other doesn't. But let's face it, it would be a lot more fun to putter together. So every once in a while, when you see your partner heading for the garden, put down what you are doing and join him or her.
- One partner adores sports, the other doesn't. The partner who is not a sports aficionado should get a pair of tickets to a game and go along, and try to join in the excitement.
- One partner is doing the laundry or taking out the garbage or putting up the storm windows—the other should jump in and join in.

Let me say something important here—this jumping in may not sit well, at least not as an initial reaction. If one person has been gardening/putting out the garbage/doing the laundry for twenty years, maybe they have a certain way of doing it. Maybe they don't think they need any help. But you're trying to reestablish the connections that have been broken over the years. So as important as it is for one partner to make the effort to jump in, it's important for the other to accept the jumpee. Once your connections have been firmly reestablished, some of this artificial togetherness can be set aside. But to establish a feeling of cooperation and camaraderie, you have to do things together, and since your days and nights can't and won't be filled with new and exciting activities, you have to use some of the everyday and commonplace ones.

Let me say this again in another way because it is an important point. Over the years you have probably placed some barriers between the two of you. You've been stressed and tense and felt that there were times when you desperately needed your own space. You or your partner made the garden or the workshop or the kitchen or the bathroom into a place to escape. Now I'm not saying that the two of you have to share gardening or cooking or showering each and every time you perform this activity for the rest of your lives. But at this point in time, you want to communicate to your partner that you want to be together as much as possible and any and every opportunity will do. But once you both feel that you've broken down those barriers and that you're communicating very well, then it's perfectly okay to go back to your old routines, at least some of the time. Hopefully you'll establish some new routines that will be ones you always share.

Ideally, the first step in this process is to discuss it so that you're both on the same page. You want to agree that you're going to try to communicate in some new ways, new times, and new places, but that you'll also both understand if these don't always work out. For example, if he's shaving and she walks in and starts talking about what he wants for dinner, which she's never done before, he may wonder what's going on. He might think to himself, "I have to concentrate here or I'm going to cut myself." Or "I really need to go over what I'm going to say at that meeting I have with the boss at 9 A.M." But instead of saying, "Hey, I'm shaving and I need some privacy," he should be sufficiently clued in to what is happening so that he can say, "Sorry honey, but I really need to think about my meeting so you decide today, but tomorrow we can try this again."

Keep in mind that no matter how much communicating you do, there's a good chance that you're going to have differing levels of expectations. What one partner may find very romantic, the other might find has almost no romance quotient at all. It may take a while for the two of you to reach a level that satisfies both of you. But you both have to be willing to compromise, of course. This is no time for the drawing of lines in the sand. You're not going into battle; you're rekindling your romance. If you find that the process is starting more fights than lovemaking, then it's time that you seek out a professional counselor who can play the role of referee.

A Word to Men

Some men have a hard time figuring out exactly what romance is. They sort of know that it's not sex, but because it can lead to sex, that can confuse them. Let me try to give you an explanation that you will understand.

To me, romance is the context in which love exists. The sounds, sights, smells, and touches that define love have to be communicated between the lovers, and this transfer needs a medium. That medium is romance.

Picture two scenarios. In the first, you're in your rattiest jeans, you're watching a football game, your wife passes by and you say, "Hey, babe, love you." In the second, you're at a restaurant with the lights turned down low, you're dressed well, even if you don't have on a jacket and tie, you take her hand across the table, you look into her eyes, and you say, "Honey, I'm so glad we met, you're the love of my life." These are obviously the extremes, but no matter how low your romantic meter is set, I believe that you can appreciate the difference. If I had to explain why in a few words, in the second example, love is obviously given so much more respect. The words *I love you* are given an importance that they're not in the first.

You can't spend your life in a romantic restaurant, and while I love candlelight, it's not appropriate 24/7. But putting love front and center is necessary once in a while, and with some regularity.

Romance isn't about spending money. Every woman loves diamonds, but it's not necessary to invest great sums of money to be romantic. What you have to invest into romance is yourself. Your concentration, your interest, your eyes, ears, hands. And if you can't give 100 percent, you have to get as close to that ideal as possible.

How often do you have to do this? Before I try to answer that, let me return to that little word *sex*. You see, romance is what gets women aroused. So the better your romantic skills, the more sex you're likely to share with your partner. So to get back to that question about how much, there's no set amount of time you have to devote to romance, but since there's a very nice payback, I would recommend setting aside the most time possible.

How to Make Romance Palatable

For whatever reason, if given the choice between watching sports on television and being romantic, most men would choose the ball game. Most women, on the other hand, would choose a romantic activity over just about anything else. Is there a way of making romance more palatable for men? Here are some ideas of how to combine your interests with romance.

The best way of doing this is to find interests that you both share, and if you don't have any, then to find some. For example, in most households, it's the women who do the cooking. And yet most chefs in restaurants are men. So here's a natural area that you could share. If you're working together to plan, shop, and prepare meals, those will be romantic times. To make sure that they are, you have to cooperate and not try to take over. And while you're cooking, you have to exchange hugs or kisses. You should say sweet things like, "I love cooking with you," and simply, "I love you." You also have to use body language so that you should look over at her and give her a wink or a smile. You have to be a bit playful, so that the time is fun. So you see, if you work at it, cooking together can be very romantic.

Many people take a nightly stroll after dinner. This is time when you're together, you're active, and you have privacy. If you hold hands or put your arms around each other, that will make it romantic. If you talk about old times and future plans instead of how much laundry there is to do or how high the bills are piled, that will be romantic. If you can watch the sunset quietly, or admire some flowers, that will be romantic.

Exercise can be romantic if you do it together. When people go to the gym to exercise, they'll often work out together, but also for safety sake, so that one person can be a spotter for the other, and to give each other encouragement. Now a man and a woman might be at different strength levels, but that doesn't mean they can't exercise together. There are some exercises where you use your strength against each other, a form of resistance training, that can give both of you a workout. There are books and tapes that spell these out and I might suggest you get one. Also, watching each other's form can be useful. But mostly it's a question of giving each other encouragement, and then when you're done, cooling down together, over a glass of cold water, and maybe even taking a shower together. If you do this twice a week, I guarantee you it will help to spark your romance.

If you like to listen to music, do it together. If it's a fast tune, you could boogie. If it's a slow song you could fall into each other's arms and slow dance. And if it's a classical or jazz piece, you could simply hold each other while curling up on the couch.

When you go to bed, don't fall asleep right away, but spend some time holding each other and feeling each other's warmth. This doesn't have to be a prelude to sex, but rather a romantic moment. And if you're exhausted at the end of the day, then get up ten minutes earlier and do it in the morning.

And here's one "negative" tip. The most unromantic item in your household is the television. It distracts you, and when you have it on while you're eating or while you're in bed, it blocks any chance of romance occurring. I'm not saying not to have a television in your house, but if you can keep it in a room devoted only to television watching, like a den, you'll be doing your romance a very big favor.

And if you're still not sure how to add some romance to your daily routine, I suggest you write down what it is you do when you're together. Analyze each activity and see if you can find ways of making them even a bit more romantic. At dinner, use smaller glasses and make a point of filling your partner's glass whenever it's empty. If you're reading the paper, check out the entertainment section and then talk about what shared activity, like going to a museum or show, you might do the next weekend. If you're the first one to open the day's mail, make a neat little stack of your partner's mail, and add a Post-it on one of the envelopes that says I Love You.

Case History: Tim and Georgia

Tim and Georgia's twenty-second wedding anniversary was coming up. Tim was wracking his brain trying to come up with the right gift. Tim remembered that their first date had been ice skating together. He went to a sporting goods store and bought his and hers skates and even arranged for the manager of the rink to agree to play "their" song. He came home from work that day, presented her with the skates, and told her to get ready to reenact their first date. Georgia, who was a third grade teacher and was on her feet all day, gave him a wan smile and told him that she'd rather skip it as she was too tired. She had been hinting at some diamond earrings that she wanted to wear to an upcoming wedding and so was very disappointed at the skates. And Tim was devastated that all his planning had been for naught.

For Women

I've been concentrating my tips for the men folk, as it seems they don't have this natural affinity for romance, but learning to adapt to their foibles on this subject can make life easier on women.

First, put aside your resentment about your man's lack of sensitivity when it comes to romance. Some women feel that unless their husbands take the lead, a moment or an activity or an evening loses any opportunity for romance. If a husband won't follow his wife's lead, then that would be true, but if your husband needs a cue, then go ahead and give it to him. If you want to dine by candlelight, then put candles on the table and light them. If flowers make you feel good, order some. If you want him to dress up for dinner, ask him to. If you want to go for a picnic in the country, tell him and ask him to help plan it.

I know there are some men who will look down their noses when their wives try to act romantic, but there are a lot more men who will play along. Remember, men voluntarily go into activities where there are strong hierarchies. In sports, business, the army, there are a few leaders and most of the others follow. So men have a certain comfort level in such situations. So when it comes to romance, where they may be a bit clueless, you take the lead and don't feel negatively about it. It's better to experience some romantic moments that you created than to have none at all.

The Role of Fantasy

Many women, when they fantasize, will drift toward fantasies where they are forced by some dark, swarthy stranger into having sex, or some variation thereof. I often get questions in the mail or on my web site from women asking me why they have such fantasies, since in real life they would never want to be forced into having sex.

The reason these types of fantasies are so common is that many women, when they were little, had the message drummed into their head that sex was bad, something only to be endured, not enjoyed. By employing a forceful, overpowering man in their fantasies, these women have given themselves permission to enjoy sex within the context of this fantasy, which they might not be able to do without such a scenario.

Some women in real life are drawn to the type of man that acts out, at least in some small way, this set of fantasies. These women usually wind up getting hurt, hopefully only emotionally but sadly, sometimes physically, and yet they will seek out the same type of man again and again. This is not a healthy situation, and most women want a man who while strong, is also loving and supportive.

Obviously, this dual need of wanting a strong-willed yet supportive man creates somewhat of a conflict. Finding the perfect man who will fulfill your darkest fantasies while he also tenderly takes care of you and your children is just about impossible. And so that's one reason why your search for romance is often not as satisfying as you would like. And that's why I'm saying to you to create romantic moments, which you can make even more romantic, perhaps, by adding a little fantasy.

I understand that it would be much better if your husband would don his Superman outfit and whisk you off on some romantic adventure, but if you set the right example for him, it might actually happen now and again (without the costume, I hope). But in order to get the ball rolling, listen to my advice and take the initiative if that's the only way for you to get some of the romance you desire into your relationship. After all, you've been together for a long time, and if his romantic initiatives have been few and far between, then you can't expect a sudden change now. But I do believe that you can teach an old dog new tricks, and the key word in that saying is *teach*. If you expect him to become more romantic by osmosis, it's probably not going to happen. But if you give him some examples of what you are looking for, then he might just surprise you with some romantic initiatives that he thought up on his very own.

Romance Doesn't Have to Be Spontaneous

There's another school of thought regarding romance that can be dangerous, and that's the credo that says true romance has to be spontaneous. To this group, planning equals artificiality. You have to be ready to seize romantic moments as they happen, not try to create them.

It's not that I'm against spontaneous romance, but you could also wait for years for the right moment and in the meantime allow a lot of potential opportunities for romance to pass you by. It's true that if your children have left, there are more occasions when you can be spontaneous, and you should grab them if possible. But just as you had to make plans to get a babysitter before you could have a romantic evening a few years earlier, you might find that it will take some planning to have some romance now as well. For example, there was a time you could party 'til the wee hours and still make it to the office and even function the next day. But now that would be quite a feat, and if you've got more responsibilities, then you've got to function at top form, not just be at your desk in body only.

So rather than always playing it by ear, sit down together and plan some romantic evenings. Don't complain about the artificiality of it, but instead enjoy the predictability. I'm not saying that you have to start out so early that you're in time for the early bird specials, but I think if you plan for dinner, it will give you both the opportunity to pace yourselves and you'll end up enjoying it more rather than less.

Case History: Bret and Eve

Eve's father, Chet, was a widower, and when his emphysema got very bad, she insisted that he come live with her and her husband, Bret. Chet couldn't really fend for himself as the least little effort left him breathless. He could have been put into a hospital, but since there was nothing that they could do for him, Eve thought he'd be happier living in a real home, at least for as long as was possible. Eve sold real estate, so on many evenings and all day Saturday and Sunday, she was out showing houses to prospective clients. When she was gone, Bret did all he could to take care of Chet. He'd fix his meals, help him get around, and watch sports events with him. Having Chet around took away much of their privacy, but the more Eve saw Bret do for her father, the more in love she fell with her husband.

The Toughness of Romance

I said earlier that romance was the medium, the ether, in which love existed, but while it is true that love and romance has an ethereal quality to it, there is also a tough side. After all, you've certainly heard that love can thrive in some pretty horrendous situations. Love has bloomed in wartime, in concentration camps, and in the aftermath of natural disasters and deadly illnesses. Just think of all the movies you've seen that have had that exact plot. Now while I wish for you only good things, we all know that some days are better than others, and some are just out and out rotten. But even the worst days can have their portion of romance. If two people have endured some sort of tragedy, that can definitely bring them closer together and strengthen their love. Now that you're in your Whitewater Years, you're going to hit some bumps in the road. We just covered a "happy" one, which happens when all you're kids leave home. You want them to be independent, but it still leaves an ache. But that you have each other to cling to makes it easier to bear, and it does bring you closer.

Some people crawl into a shell when they run into trouble. Following that path will only damage your relationship. But if you allow the bad as well as the good to bring you together, your love will grow even stronger. Allowing your partner to share your pain or suffering forms a stronger bond. An important component of love is trust. If you show that you trust your partner when you're at your weakest, when you're most vulnerable, you'll find that it's a potentially very intimate moment. Much more intimate than when you're both bursting with joy. It's the feeling that you might get holding a little bird in your hand. Your heart can't help but go out to it.

As the years go on, you'll find that there may be more of these vulnerable moments than you'd wish. But by sealing the bond between you during the Whitewater Years, they'll be a lot easier to face and to overcome.

Second Honeymoons

One of the rituals that many couples go through in their Whitewater Years in the second honeymoon. If you got married when you were between twenty-five and thirty-five, then your twenty-fifth wedding anniversary will fall in prime Whitewater Years.

As you might imagine, I'm all in favor of any chance to give your relationship a boost, and second honeymoons can certainly do that, but there are also a few pitfalls that I want to caution you about.

The first has to do with expectations. It's important that you're both on the same page when planning such an event. Even though you know that it can't possibly be an exact replica of your first honeymoon, some people await just that outcome. On the other hand, some spouses look at it as just another vacation, and if there's a good opportunity to play golf or to shop, they see no reason not to go off and enjoy themselves at their favorite sport. If you haven't told each other your hopes for this trip, then one of you may get very disappointed, and this disappointment may get magnified because of the occasion. So make sure that you do talk about what you would like to get out of this voyage, even if it's not a particularly elaborate one, so that you avoid unnecessary disappointment.

My second warning has to do with your physical health. You're a lot older than you were the first time and you have to remember to act your age. Otherwise one or both of you may find yourselves laid up, and that will ruin everything. A little moderation in terms of eating, drinking, taking in the sun, and, yes, having sex may serve you very well.

Finally, some couples feel a great let down after returning from a second honeymoon. It's something they may have been planning for years, but afterward, what is there to plan for? If you're looking at the same old routine for as far as the eye can see, then you could see that it might make you depressed. So my advice is to look at this second honeymoon as the start of a new life together. While you're on this vacation, make plans for the next one, or plans about anything else that might get you excited. That way when you come home it will be with a sense of looking forward to future good times rather than one of having had all the fun you're entitled to.

CHAPTER **9**

When the Relationship Turns Sour

I'VE BEEN TRYING TO HELP YOU AVOID THE ROCKS in the rapids of the Whitewater Years, but what happens if you or your spouse hit one? It doesn't have to lead to the end of the relationship, but it could. In this chapter I want to go over what can happen when the relationship goes sour as well as discuss what you can do about it.

Since I'm a sex therapist and see clients who have either sexual or marital relationship problems, from my perspective the biggest, most jagged rock that your kayak might hit is the extramarital affair. Do these exist? Absolutely. Do I believe all the statistics I read about how many affairs people have? Not exactly. When it comes to sex, I know that people lie. Or should I say, exaggerate. After all, if a pollster came up to you and asked you how many people you'd slept with and the answer was actually one or maybe two, wouldn't you be tempted to throw a few more in there? On the other hand, the divorce rate is a real statistic, so most certainly there are married people who cheat on their spouses and that leads to their marriages falling apart.

Not every divorce is caused by an affair, and not every affair causes a divorce. The marriage is more likely to end in divorce after an affair is revealed if the couple's relationship was already in bad shape, so that the news of the affair becomes the final straw and not necessarily the main reason the couple splits up. And by affair, I'm only including those couplings that turn into a regular series of events. Lots of people have one-night stands while on business trips or whatever, but those may never come to light and so don't end up causing a divorce, though if they are discovered, they too can certainly represent a significant danger to a marriage.

Horns of a Dilemma

I get many letters from people who tell me that they love their spouses but they find themselves in the middle of an affair and don't know what to do about it. They don't want to wreck their marriage, but the attraction for this other person is too strong for them to just give it up. Are these people lying, or do they really love their spouses despite their sexual activities outside the marriage? The truth can be hard to discern, but the only way to get at the truth is for the person to put aside the affair and see if he or she can fix the marriage, because obviously something is wrong.

Case History: Jim and Carol, Part 1

Jim and Carol have been married for twenty-three years. Carol does love Jim, but their sex life has been in the doldrums for more than a decade. Jim was always very busy at his job, putting in long hours, and they tended to only have sex on the weekends, and even that was often perfunctory and not very satisfying. When a slightly younger man at Carol's office starting paying attention to her, she ended up not being able to resist the temptation of having sex with him. And when the sex turned out to be so much more intense than anything she had ever experienced with Jim, it turned into a regular occurrence. The other man wasn't married, and he started to put growing demands on her time, so that Carol knew she wouldn't be able to hide the affair for much longer. It was time to choose but she couldn't make up her mind. Her children were out of the house so that wasn't an excuse she could use to end the affair, and she couldn't see herself going back to having a sex life that left her so unsatisfied, especially now that she knew what good sex offered.

Someone in Carol's predicament has to separate the two relationships. She has to put aside the affair and try to fix her marriage. Her husband has to wake up to the fact that his marriage is in danger. It's possible he won't take this information seriously and then Carol can make the decision to end it. Or they might be able to reignite the spark that was once there, and the decision to stay married will become easy. But for there to be any chance of saving this marriage, Carol has to take action, otherwise the affair will continue for so long that it will eat away at the marriage to the point where the marriage will not be salvageable.

Why Men Have Affairs

As I mentioned earlier in chapter 4, a common cause for an affair is the man's ignorance of the fact that it is entirely normal for him to lose the ability to have psychogenic erections. Many men, when they stop having erections that come without any physical contact, decide that they are no longer attracted to their wives and they begin to look for that sexual stimulation elsewhere. As I said, that may work for a time, but not forever, and this new, younger woman is not going to be as forgiving as a long-term wife when his erections once again lose some of their strength, unless, of course, she's in it only for the money.

Certainly not every man who goes through this ends up having an affair, but let me say to all you women readers out there, my advice is not to risk it. If you notice that your husband is no longer becoming erect at times when he used to automatically, then you should start paying a bit more attention to his penis. Remember, it's not that he cannot have an erection, but only that he needs a little help. Now if you've seen how loathe he is to ask for help in most instances, especially when he's behind the wheel of a car, an activity not quite as filled with machismo as having sex but a close second, then you can assume that he's not going to be comfortable asking you to help him have erections. But if you volunteer, that's another story.

What do I mean by volunteer? Let's take the minimum scenario. Every Friday night the two of you used to have sex. Then, suddenly, or gradually, it stops, and it's not replaced by sex at some other time. You could act hurt and do nothing about this, or, on Friday nights, you could cuddle up against your husband at some point and put your hand on his crotch. This could be before you're even undressed. By touching his penis, you will give him the stimulation he requires to have an erection. Then your Friday night sex life will be able to resume.

But as I said earlier, having an erection promotes good health in a man's penis. The more erections he has, the more he'll be able to have. So why not help give him erections at times when it won't necessarily translate into having sex immediately. This will have two benefits: the health benefit that I just mentioned and an increase in your overall intimacy. Many women who used to fondle their husbands' penises early on in the relationship stop doing so because it signals that they want to have sex, and once children arrive along with other responsibilities, they don't have time in the middle of the day, or maybe even in the middle of the week, to have sex. But if you explain to him what you're going to be doing and why, and then you do it at times when sex is not possible, such as under the table at a restaurant, he'll learn to appreciate this attention. And it will pay off at other times when the two of you do have sex, as you'll both be comfortable with your giving him erections. This type of behavior will also help to inoculate your marriage against the dangers of an affair, for if you've taken this responsibility for your husband's sexual enjoyment, then it's less likely that those duties will go to someone else.

Oral Sex

Up to this point I've been using the terms *fondle* or *stimulate*, but I haven't really discussed another way to please a man, and that's oral sex. Among younger people, oral sex has become no big deal. Many young people who want to remain virgins use oral sex as a substitute, and whether or not you want to consider two people who regularly engage in oral sex as virgins or not, it definitely becomes part of their sexual repertoire for the rest of their lives. But for people now in their Whitewater Years, oral sex may or may not be something that they've done. I know that a great many men would enjoy having oral sex performed on them, but I also know that there are a lot of women for whom this act is distasteful.

I don't believe in putting pressure on anyone, and I certainly don't want to put any pressure on a woman in her Whitewater Years to perform oral sex if she doesn't want to. But I also have to be honest. If an older married man does have an affair with a younger woman, there's a very good chance that she's going to give him oral sex. In fact, if she's one of those who considers herself a virgin at a time when she was having only oral sex, she might not even think of it as that big of a deal if she was giving some man oral sex but not having intercourse. But if this man is of the previous generation, and oral sex was something that he had longed for from his wife but never received, then you can see how this might cause trouble. In this type of situation, he's in seventh heaven while the young lady in question doesn't even think that she's having sex. And this is occurring at a time when he is actually in need of added physical stimulation.

So, while I'm not putting pressure on you women, remember, I might suggest that you think about the subject. And let me say one more thing about oral sex. Many women who object to oral sex do so because they really don't like the idea of the man ejaculating in their mouths. When giving oral sex to an older man, the odds of this happening by accident are a lot smaller. A young man to whom a woman is giving oral sex will already have an erection, while an older gentleman is looking to the oral sex to get an erection. It will also take him longer to have an orgasm than a younger man, and so if you agree to use oral sex to get him aroused but not to bring him to orgasm, the issue of getting his ejaculate in your mouth, apart from the few drops of Cowper's fluid that leaks from a man's penis before he ejaculates, should not be an issue. That's not to say that he wouldn't enjoy it if you did continue until he ejaculated, but only that if you don't want to, it's probably not going to happen accidentally.

Male Issues

But as we all know, even mild erectile difficulties aren't the only reason that a man has an affair. A wife can be the best lover there is and her husband might still fool around. (Of course there are men who start fooling around early in the marriage and never stop. That's the subject for another book. Here we're only covering why this might occur during the Whitewater Years.) Some men may want to relive their youth. Others are looking for so-called arm candy. For some it's a result of empty-nest syndrome, as they decide that they really don't love their wives anymore and so fall into the arms of someone else while they remain married rather than separating first. Some men are simply lured by another woman and get trapped into having an affair. There are those who miss what is sometimes referred to as "the hunt" and just want to prove to themselves that they've still got "it" and can attract a woman into bed with them. Some men spend a lot of time on the road and just give in to temptation. Some men get depressed by the thought of growing older and turn to sex to perk themselves up the way others turn to alcohol or drugs. Others run into an old girlfriend and decide that they miss what they lost so long ago.

As you can see, there are many, many possible scenarios as to why a man might have an affair. In many cases, there's not much a wife can do about it. The circumstances are beyond her control and deciding to forgive him, assuming he wants that, or asking for a divorce are the only options left. But knowing that there are so many potential traps should give a wife the incentive to make a little bit of an extra effort. You shouldn't assume that because you have been married for twenty years that there is no competition out there for your man. Now I'm not suggesting that you go in the opposite direction and start acting like a possessive, jealous woman. That's more likely to drive a man away than keep him from straying. What I am saying is that you should not assume that now that the two of you have reached the home stretch, so to speak, that everything is going to go smoothly.

You have to take an active role for your love life to survive, even if it is going to go somewhat downhill as you both age. You have to put in enough energy and creativity to slow down any reduction in your sex life so that it doesn't result in pulling you apart.

What's a Wife to Do?

So what can you do? I'm glad you asked. Here are some suggestions that you should take as guidelines, adapting them to your own unique situation.

Many women who are approaching or have already gone through menopause put on some weight. As I've said, since fat cells produce hormones, adding fat is one way your body fights off the effects of menopause. It's tough keeping that weight off, but often some of that weight shows up in your breasts, and most men will appreciate that aspect. So one thing you can do is show them off to him in both subtle and not so subtle ways. And be sexy in general. Not every second of the day, but don't let days and weeks go by where you're not acting sexy either. Keeping him interested in you sexually is an important component of your marriage.

As I've said over and over, boredom can kill any relationship. Do whatever you can to sweep boredom aside. Make yourself interesting and find interesting things for the two of you to do.

If you have a health problem, either physical or mental, do something about it. Don't assume that any aches or pains or stress or depression are a result of your age and can't be helped. Get professional help so that you are in the best shape you can be.

Stay active. That certainly includes exercise and sports, hopefully some that you can do with your husband. But it also means filling your days with worthwhile activities. If you have a job, then this advice may not apply, as you're quite active as it is, but if you don't, then get involved in some form of charity work that gets you out of the house and makes you less dependent on your husband. That will actually improve your relationship.

Take some risks. As we get older, it's easy to fall into a rut. But a relationship needs some surprises to stay vibrant. So cook something you've never made before. Go someplace unexpected. Wear an outfit that's "not you." Go to see a movie or a play that's not your normal fare. Make a dinner date with people you barely know. Keep him guessing, not all of the time but some of the time, and your relationship will benefit.

Listen. In general, women talk more than men. Sometimes it seems women talk just to fill in any gaps, as if silence were something negative. After a while, men will just turn off to such chattering and won't bother trying to get a word in themselves. If you think this applies to you, then make a point of keeping your mouth shut once in a while. Your husband may surprise you by opening his, and if you are careful, you may be able to reestablish reciprocal communication, which is vital to the health of any relationship.

Be aware and vigilant. I don't want you to become paranoid, but you also shouldn't be oblivious. Very often there are signs that something is wrong in a relationship, and the earlier you can catch those signs and fix whatever is wrong, the likelier that the relationship will survive. I'm not only speaking of an actual affair, because by the time you discover that, it may well be too late. But if you're not speaking to each other or if your sex life has disappeared or you never kiss, that should raise your antenna. Don't shrug these problems off, but try to get to the bottom of them as soon as possible.

When Women Stray

I've been addressing the reasons that men have affairs, but men are not the only partners that will wander off. Obviously it takes two to tango, and every man having an affair isn't doing so with a single woman. There are lots of married women who get together with married men, and single men too.

While the physical component seems to be more important in driving a man to seek sex elsewhere, it's most definitely also part of the reason that women stray. A woman might put more emphasis on the emotional aspect of an affair, which is why the ratio of female to male prostitutes is so overwhelming, as men can easily enjoy sex without any relationship at all, but there has to be a sexual quotient for women as well. In fact, while she might not be orgasmic with her husband, if a woman is going to have an affair, she most likely will get quite a lot of sexual satisfaction from this new man. A woman who was in a marriage where very little sex was taking place is likely to have had fewer outside sexual outlets than a man in the same position. Men will, at the very least, masturbate, while fewer women will take that route, if for no other reason than women need more time and privacy to masturbate. So if a woman is starved for love and sex, when she finds it she's likely to find herself very interested in that aspect of the affair.

Case History: Jim and Carol, Part 2

Carol and Jim went to see a sex therapist and for a time their marriage seemed to be back on track. There was an improvement in their sex life, though not to the level of the sex she had during the affair, but since Carol really didn't want to break up her marriage, she put up with it. But after six months, she gave in to the pleadings of her former lover and met him for dinner. She discovered that it wasn't only the sex that she missed, but the way that he treated her. He made her feel like someone really special, and before she knew what was happening, she had resumed the affair.

For a woman to enjoy sex, she needs to feel sexy. It's easy for a husband who has spent twenty or more years with a woman to think of his wife as more of a friend than a lover. Men require less stimulation to become aroused than women. Even if an older man needs a bit more, arousal can still grow to the point where he desires sex in a matter of minutes. However, the longer a woman has to become aroused, the higher her level of arousal is likely to be. And all those little compliments, sweet words, and other forms of attention that a man can pay a woman during the course of the day serve to arouse her, at least on a potential level, so that when it is time to have sex, she will be much more excited than she would otherwise be. While Jim was trying, he found it difficult to change his behavior after so many years. Of course, if he'd been after some new woman he'd know how to act, so this resistance is artificial. It doesn't take much effort to give your wife a compliment or a hug, but too many men appear to not want to be bothered.

One reason for this is that they have no role models. In all likelihood, their fathers didn't show their mothers much affection. Much as with movies or television, you need to have conflict to make an interesting show. If everything is going well, what can the writers come up with as a plot? So instead of showing men who treat their wives the way wives would like to be treated, we're surrounded by examples of what not to do.

Another has to do with control. These men feel that if they treat their wives the way they want to be treated they are somehow being forced into this and so are giving up control. They say to themselves that they'd give a compliment if it was entirely their idea, but then the opportunity never seems to come up and the words never leave their mouths.

That women give each other compliments so easily also makes men more reticent. Men don't understand how a woman can gush over another woman's outfit or a hairstyle, so men see the whole concept of compliments as something silly.

And young men make a point of not giving each other compliments, other than a high five for a well made shot at some sport, but instead make a game of putting each other down. After years of such play, it can be difficult for a man to switch gears and start giving compliments.

This is mostly an American attitude, which is why European men are so much better at giving compliments. It stems from the frontier spirit, where I suppose opportunities for speaking were fewer, assuming you didn't want to talk to the cattle, and somehow this attitude carries on to this day.

Another problem has to do with the way love has been marketed. To retailers, the best way for a man to prove his love is to spend the most amount of money, as that is the way that they make the most amount of money. Retailers create ads pushing this type of consumption, and this resonates with men because it sets up a competition—which guy on the block can give his wife the biggest diamond—and men like to compete. And when women pick up on this idea, which they do because they'd rather have a gift than nothing, then it becomes a self-fulfilling mode of exchange.

So how does a man turn this situation around and learn to treat his wife as a lover instead of a companion? First of all, he has to change his attitude toward compliments in general. He has to be able to differentiate between a real compliment and a fake one, and develop the instinct to let those real ones come out of his mouth rather than automatically stuffing them back inside.

He should also remind himself, as frequently as possible, that he shouldn't take his wife for granted. Many men take better care of their cars than their wives. They remember to change the oil regularly and wash it and fill the tank, but they'll ignore their wives' needs entirely. So just think of these compliments and kind words directed at your wife as regular tune-ups for your relationship. And keep in mind, that if you fail to give them to her, it's possible that she may be lured away by some other guy.

And it wouldn't be a bad thing to learn how to give compliments generally. If you have people who work under you, telling them that they've done a good job, when it's deserved, will go a long way toward building loyalty.

What if your wife has put on more weight than you find attractive and you just can't find it in yourself to pay her a compliment? First of all, there are plenty of compliments you can give that have nothing to do with her weight. You can compliment her on a good meal, or a good job in any type of activity. (By the way, words of thanks can act as compliments, so that while you would appear foolish telling her what a good job she did with the laundry, saying thank you would provide its own form of satisfaction.) You can also compliment her for what she is wearing, or how she smells, or the way she styled her hair. And compliments will also serve to help her take action with regard to her weight, while a lack of compliments may send her to the candy dish for solace.

Some men not only don't give compliments, but they actually say derogatory things about their wives in public. It should be obvious that such nastiness is not going to earn you any Brownie points, even if it's in jest. There are plenty of things to joke about without launching barbs at your wife. If you're not sure whether or not you do this, think back on the last time you were out with some friends. You may find that it's become an unconscious habit. If that's the case, then you have to grab control of your mouth and keep any such jokes from escaping.

And for you strong silent types, there are plenty of ways of complimenting and showing attention to your wife that don't require a lot of words. First of all, a compliment doesn't require a soliloquy. "You look great" says a lot, as do "Thanks" and "I love you." And when words elude you entirely, a hug is good, as is a kiss that's more than a peck or taking her hand. Opening doors says a lot. Helping with dinner preparation and clean up says even more. And for my personal all-time favorite, there's always a nice massage. It can be a quickie or, better yet, a long drawn-out affair.

If It's Too Late

What if you're too late in changing your ways and she's sought comfort with someone else? If you're the type who would want an instant separation, then that's your choice. But what if you do love her and don't want to see the marriage fall apart? Is there anything that you can do?

The absolute best thing you can do is to go for professional help. Whether your wife agrees to accompany you or not, you must seek out a marital therapist. It's no different than going to an orthopedic surgeon if you break your leg. Yes, your leg might heal without the doctor's help, but you also might never walk again. Whether or not the therapist can rescue the marriage, you should come out of the experience in better shape than without this type of guidance.

Going for help also sends out a strong signal to your spouse. It says that you are serious about wanting her back and that you're willing to make changes in the marriage if she does come back. That's not to say that she won't have to make changes also, but you have to admit that the marriage has been shattered and that you know the two of you are not going to go back to exactly the same marriage you had before. It may end up being a better marriage, but your relationship will undergo some serious alterations if it's going to be successful. Some couples get back together but don't make the necessary adjustments, and sooner or later they split up again. As far as I'm concerned, that's a waste. Of all the variables of life, time is the one over which you have the least control, and you have to learn to make the most of every minute, even every second. So going back into a marriage that is undoubtedly doomed is the wrong move, in my book. If you're not willing to make adjustments so that the marriage has a chance, then you're better off ending it and starting the search for a new partner.

Case History: Bill and Susan

Susan kept rising through the ranks of her law firm and had become a senior partner. It seemed that Bill's ego couldn't take that and he would constantly pick on her at home for the least little "mistake" she made. She hated going home and would almost always work late. Another male partner was often there with her and one thing led to another and they had an affair. Bill felt very hurt and insisted that she move out. Susan moved into a studio apartment with too few closets and so continued to leave many of her clothes and other belongings in the old apartment. When she would go over to get something, she and Bill would talk, and before she knew what has happening, they would end up having sex. The man she was having the affair with had broken it off, scared by Bill's reaction to thinking he might lose his wife. Susan had asked Bill if he wanted her to move back in, but he refused, and yet they continued to have sex almost once a week.

You might think that people who'd decided to end a marriage, either through separation or divorce, would never want to have sex again, but this is not always true. For some couples there is a chemistry that never disappears, so whether or not the two people feel that they can live together, they can't seem to keep their hands off each other.

As I just said, my philosophy is against wasting time. If a relationship isn't moving forward, then you should end it and move forward by yourself into a new relationship. Situations like the one that Bill and Susan find themselves in are a terrible waste of time. Neither partner feels entirely free to find someone new, and yet they are giving up months and maybe even years of their lives literally going nowhere.

Ending a relationship is a very hard thing to do. The pain can be severe and it's easy to understand that the people involved might try to soften the blow. But even though the pain may appear to be lessened by an extended breakup period, drawing it out actually means that in the long run, each partner suffers more pain. Small doses may appear to be easy to swallow, but since they prevent you from advancing to the next relationship, which hopefully will be a better one, it's a mistake to put off the final breakup.

And when the delaying tactics include sex, that can be an even bigger mistake. Sexual tension can definitely drive you toward finding a new partner. Eliminating that sexual tension by having sex with your ex therefore exacerbates this difficult situation. So while it may be tempting to comfort yourself from the effects of a breakup by sleeping with the person you're breaking up with, this contradiction in terms is also contraindicated.

CHAPTER **10**

Other Pitfalls

J UST AS THERE ARE DANGERS AROUND EVERY BEND of a raging river, our everyday lives are sur-rounded by danger—behemoth trucks on the highways, germs floating in the air, bosses prone to temper tantrums—though luckily for most of us, we manage to skirt around the edges and paddle our way safely through each day. But the longer we live, the higher the odds that we will fall into one of these traps. I'm not going to touch on every one of these, because not only would I depress you, my readers, but I'd depress myself. But there are some that deserve attention in this book as they fit into areas of my expertise.

The first one I want to address is pornography. While this is not a problem that is limited to people in their White-water Years, many of the people who ask me about it do come from that age range. The questions most often come from wives whose husbands can't seem to get enough of this type of material, often ignoring their wives because of it.

There have been two big changes in pornography. The first came when every home got a VCR that allowed the viewing of films that before one could only see in a limited number of theaters. But while erotic videos certainly have a lure, even they can't compare to what's available on the Internet.

Case History: Steve and Alice

There had been a computer in Steve and Alice's home for many years, but when their teenage children were around, it was difficult for the parents to get on it. But once they were both off to college, the computer was freed up, and with no young people likely to peer over his shoulder, Steve used it to look at web sites that featured Asian women without their clothes on. Steve would pretend that he was doing work on the computer, but once his wife went to bed, he'd go online and go to his favorite sites. One night Alice got up and caught him and he claimed that he had just been curious. But the next day, Alice looked at the computer's history and saw that he'd been visiting those sites regularly for months. She also came to the realization that their sex life had gone on the wane during this time as well.

Undoubtedly part of men's psyches are linked to hunting. There are many men who go after women and drop them as soon as they have sex with them. When it comes to erotica and the Internet, the hunting instinct again seems to take over. While a woman would definitely get bored seeing the same type of erotic images over and over, men seem to enjoy looking for just that special picture, even if it means combing through pages and pages of erotica where one is no different from all the rest. And that is a big part of the problem, for they end up spending hours staring at their computer screens, completely ignoring live women who are available to them—their wives.

I think that in many cases where this occurs, the relationship already had problems. Perhaps the couple's sex life wasn't going very well so the man turned to erotica instead. But that's definitely not always so. Some men love their wives but just find it easier to masturbate than to have sex, especially if their wives need a certain amount of time to have their own orgasms. Or maybe the man has problems with premature ejaculation and would rather not have to deal with it. And there are men who, as they enter their Whitewater Years, find that their erections need some physical prodding, and rather than ask their wives for help, they turn to masturbation.

As with any obsession, these individuals might not know that they were going to become hooked before they began. Notice I didn't use the word *addiction*. I'm not sure that word applies to this area, but the behavior is certainly one that the person has great difficulties kicking.

Now many wives object to a man even bringing home a copy of *Playboy*. They feel that their man should be totally satisfied with their bodies and they take exception to any form of competition, especially when it's a body that's young, perfect, and air-brushed. I understand this attitude, but there is another side to erotica. If by looking at these photographs of naked women a husband becomes aroused and he then turns to his wife for sex, she could benefit from it. But still, as a woman gets older, one can certainly understand not wanting to have one's body competing with all these nubile young women.

While it's certainly possible for a wife to ban the overt use of erotica from her home, that doesn't mean that she's managed to ban it from her husband's life. In the first place, he's going to see plenty of women just walking down the street, and these days women aren't covering themselves from head to toe. Remember, even in the days when women did wear layers and layers of clothing, just the sight of a woman's ankle was enough to get a man aroused. And, of course, a man has plenty of opportunities to look at erotica without his wife ever knowing.

Should women just "get over it"? The problem with taking a complete laissez-faire attitude could be that their husbands will go over the edge and spend all their spare time looking at pictures of naked women. On the other hand, making a big fuss about this issue may not be productive either because deep down you can't change the nature of a man, or a woman.

I hate to leave you in suspense, but I'm going to switch gears right here. You see while I hear from wives complaining about their husbands looking at erotica, I also hear about other couples where it's the wives who get involved on the Net, but rather than looking at images, they're hooked on chat rooms. They'll engage in cybersex, that is to say, they'll masturbate while chatting with some man that they've never met.

The difference is that some husbands like it when they discover their wives in these situations, as it makes them excited, while most women will at best tolerate their husbands' cybersex activities, and most abhor it. But, of course, it's only when it's a problem that it is a problem. If neither partner cared, or if both enjoyed their partner's extracurricular cybersex life, then there'd be nothing wrong with it. You can't cause an unintended pregnancy or catch a sexually transmitted disease masturbating, so the danger is purely psychological. But nevertheless, this type of issue can be serious enough to break up a marriage.

So what is the answer? Do we just accept cybersex the way we've come to accept e-mail and cybershopping? Or is it something that society should combat? To some degree the answer has to be subjective. Every person is going to have his or her own perspective on how much cybersex, or use of any type of erotica, is too much. But I don't think that the answer should be to have zero tolerance. After all, the basis for erotic images is the human body, so how awful can pictures of naked people be? Personally I think that the amount of violence that we show in the movies and on television, and the casual way that it is used, is much worse than showing naked people in pictures.

I wrote a book titled *The Art of Arousal*. I wrote it with a curator of the Metropolitan Museum of Art, and it's full of images, most from classic art that are quite tasteful, though there are some with more erotic content. I'm quite proud of this book, and I certainly wouldn't want to see it banned, but as tame as it is, I also wouldn't want to force anyone to leaf through its pages. I wrote it as a book that couples could look at together so as to get an appreciation of the eroticism in art. I think it might arouse both of them without making either one uncomfortable, and I'm all for that. But where *The Art of Arousal* stands on one edge of the erotic arena, cyberporn is at the other, and much of that is too far over the edge.

So practically speaking, what should you do when faced with a partner who regularly turns to cyberporn or any other erotica for sexual satisfaction? First you have to decide whether or not this impacts your sex life. If you feel that you're getting enough sex, and your partner needs more and is getting it by masturbating to pornography, then you should probably try to ignore it. If it bothers you, then you should tell your partner to be more secretive, and you should make an effort to look the other way. If the thought alone is something that you can't stand, then perhaps you'll both have to go for counseling.

More serious an issue is when you feel abandoned and are not getting the attention, sexual and otherwise, from your spouse because he or she has become hooked on cyber-sex or some other form of erotica. As I said earlier, when that happens, it might be because the relationship was already in

185

trouble, but in any case, it is definitely in trouble if you feel bad about it and your partner won't or can't stop. I don't want to say that it's an automatic cause for breaking apart because the glue that holds a couple together is a complex substance and having one area of disagreement might not be enough to break them apart, but it could.

This type of problem will probably lead to much bickering. The person who is hooked on erotica is going to feel guilty, but at the same time, he or she will have a hard time giving it up. In a sense, this person is caught in the middle between their obsessive behavior and their guilt. Since they're going to have a hard time resolving this, they might just deny it, even though the problem is quite obvious. When someone refuses to even discuss a problem, the other partner is in a tough situation. If all you do is fight over it, that's certainly not going to make for a productive relationship. But if ignoring it just leaves that person feeling all alone and abandoned, that's no better.

When you've reached the end of the line, then you have to go for professional help. It doesn't matter if your spouse agrees to go or not, as seeing a therapist will certainly begin to help you. And if the final result will be a split, then having a therapist help you through this difficult time will be very important.

Alcohol Abuse

I'm not an expert on alcoholism, but since sometimes this disease worsens during the Whitewater Years, I feel I must address it.

People often turn to alcohol when they can't deal with reality. Now there are many functioning alcoholics, people who have to drink but can manage to hold together a job and a family despite their drinking. Some manage to do this by drinking heavily only on the weekends, while others drink just enough to obliterate reality when they get home but not so much that they can't get to their jobs the next day. However, many of these people can only handle a certain amount of stress. They're coping with this mixture of normality and drunkenness, but barely. When they hit a trouble spot, and the Whitewater Years qualify as that, they may go over the edge.

Another reason the Whitewater Years worsen a problem with alcohol is that while a younger body can physically take the battering of alcohol, after decades of abusing alcohol, that body begins to break down. The liver is the classic organ to begin failing, but there's also damage done to the entire nervous system, including the brain and the heart.

Combine the physical distress with the psychological turmoil of the Whitewater Years and many alcoholics go into a tailspin. When the children leave home, a major brake is removed. An alcoholic who felt ashamed of acting drunk in front of his or her children may begin drinking more since that inhibitor is gone. And if they are no longer forced to support their children, that gives them another excuse to increase their drinking. If they feel added pressure at work from younger employees trying to move up the ladder, they may start drinking during the day as well. Soon they can no longer function at their jobs, and their relationship with their spouses is severely affected.

Alcoholism, in fact any addiction, is better treated sooner rather than later. By having allowed it to continue for such a long time, a spouse may find that it may not be reversible. The alcoholic may go through a continuing series of binges followed by enforced periods of drying out at some clinic. If your spouse is an alcoholic, you should be aware of the extra pressures that he or she will be encountering when entering the Whitewater Years. If you haven't put any pressure on your spouse to get help, it would be better to start before things get out of hand rather than after the fact. I know there are some people who believe that an alcoholic has to reach rock bottom before he or she will agree to go for help, but I don't agree with that philosophy. I don't think you are doing anyone a favor to wait for that person to sink to some terrible low. If you can intervene before that, they'll have more strength to be able to fight this disease. If you wait until they're a broken person, even if you do manage to get them to kick their habit, they may wind up being a sorry shell of the person you married. If you can save them before they reach this low point, you might end up with someone you actually want to be with. So stay on the lookout for signs of trouble, especially those caused by the Whitewater Years, and as soon as something becomes evident, begin doing something about it.

And if you do manage to get your troubled spouse into a program, don't hesitate to get some help for yourself. It's not going to be easy and not only will a counselor give you the information you need to increase the program's success, but they've seen the problems that other spouses have encountered and they'll be able to offer you some good advice as well.

Of course, no matter when you begin this process, it might prove to be too late. It's possible that the addicted person is too far gone and doesn't have the ability to break whatever addiction he or she has. (I'm including addiction to other drugs here as well as alcohol, though many more people addicted to other drugs will not have made it as far as their Whitewater Years, at least from what I've noticed.) The added difficulty this puts on a spouse is that of guilt. The likely outcome of a separation will be that the alcoholic will sink even farther into the abyss. Since you swore to stay together in sickness and in health, can you abandon someone whose disease is alcoholism?

There is no easy answer to this question. But I don't believe the only answer is to stay together either. Many alcoholics are abusive and no one would blame you for leaving in order to protect your physical well-being. Is it that much different if you leave to protect the state of your mental health? I do believe that you should do all that you can to help an addict. You should do everything in your power to convince them to go for help. You shouldn't give up after the second or third or fourth time. But I also don't believe that you have to stay forever. I'm not saying to leave because that will give the alcoholic the incentive to change. As I told you, I don't believe in that type of logic. I'm suggesting that you leave to protect yourself.

Everybody has a different breaking point. There are some people who could handle living with an alcoholic until their dying day, suffering only minimal damage to themselves. But others won't be able to and need to abandon their spouses to save themselves. And that's one of the things a counselor can help you with. They've seen it all, and they can guide you as to whether or not you've reached a level of damage where it's time to save yourself. As the spouse of an addict, you will suffer, but you're not required to suffer needlessly or endlessly.

Finances of Love

The Beatles sang "Can't Buy Me Love" and it's true that you can't put a price tag on love, but it's equally true that financial matters can definitely put a crimp in a relationship. One might think that by the time you've reached your Whitewater Years that the two of you would have figured out how to resolve conflicts about monetary issues, but that's definitely not always the case, and sometimes these issues can come to the fore and become much worse.

The Whitewater Years are when you seriously start thinking about retirement. You may have been saving for a rainy day all along, but if you're like most people, it's hard to pay close attention to what the future will be twenty years down the road. But when retirement may be less than a decade away, it's definitely time to look ahead. And where conflict arises is when two fortune tellers come up with two different visions.

The basic conflict that arises is when the nature of the two individuals resembles that of the grasshopper and the ant in Aesop's famous fable. One is a saver while the other doesn't worry so much about the future. To the saver, there can never be too much money socked away for the day when the flow of incomes will cease; while to the one who prefers the grasshopper's philosophy, his or her attitude is why save for a future that might never come.

As with every other conflict that arises between two people, the only answer is compromise. The good thing about financial issues is that they can be easily quantified so that you both can put an exact amount on how much of your income can be spent and how much should be saved. I would suggest having regular meetings, say once a quarter, to discuss this, and perhaps even putting down on paper the conclusions you reach. That way neither your spending nor your saving habits can get out of hand.

The Dreaded Pink Slip

Of course the best-laid plans will go very far awry if one of you loses a job. What makes matters worse when this happens to someone in the Whitewater Years is that it may be very difficult to get another job that pays as well as the one that's been lost. As I mentioned earlier, many firms decide that they could get somebody younger, and cheaper, to do the job done by someone in their fifties who has been with a firm for a long time and whose years at the company have earned him or her a top salary and great benefits. Some companies will even axe employees just before they attain the threshold where their retirement benefits will be at their maximum and locked in. This, of course, is disgusting, but it's becoming more and more common so it's not a problem you can altogether ignore, especially if it hits your family.

Case History: Brian and Patricia

Brian worked as the branch manager of a bank. He'd been with the bank for over twenty years and thought he was doing a good job. He knew a great many of the people who came in and his greeting was an important reason why they kept their money there. But the bank merged with another and the new management decided that Brian, and his salary, were no longer required. Brian was one of hundreds that were let go, which meant the job market in his area for people with banking skills was flooded. The only jobs that Brian could have gotten paid just above the minimum wage. Without being able to earn a weekly paycheck that fit his qualifications, Brian felt that he'd been emasculated. He was a can-do sort of guy, but there was nothing that he could do about this situation short of packing his family up and moving to another city. He became very depressed and withdrew into a shell. Patricia, his wife, tried to draw him out, but the more she intervened, the farther into his shell he went. He started to go to bed earlier and earlier and months went by without their even so much as kissing on the lips, no less making love.

When a man loses his job, it will almost always affect his libido. A man is brought up with the ideal that he is supposed to be the financial supporter of his family and if that role is taken away from him, his manhood, in whatever form it takes, will be crushed. And if it appears that this is a permanent situation, at least as far as regaining a job that will pay him at a level that is close to his old salary, then the blow will be even worse.

The most important method of treating this reaction is to expect it. If both halves of the couple know what is going on, then it should not lead to miscommunications. He'll feel less pressure if he knows she understands, and she won't feel less desirable if she knows that it's the loss of his job that is the problem. But this situation can't last forever. At some point he's going to have to allow himself to be seduced by his partner's charms. In many cases, after the initial shock has worn off, that is exactly what happens. Some men even take great comfort in the fact that they can still perform in bed.

If the two of you really can't seem to find a way of jump-starting your love life, then a trip to a sex therapist would be recommended. Sex therapy generally doesn't require too many sessions and such a situation should be looked at as an investment in your future as a couple rather than just a further drain on your already strained finances.

She's Working, He's Not

This type of situation may become more complicated if the husband loses his job and the wife still has a high-paying job. Such circumstances could definitely increase the impact that the loss of his job might have on his ego and therefore his libido. While it might appear rational to take comfort that their finances were still in decent shape because of the wife's job, men aren't always rational when it comes to this area, at least not yet anyway. Some men in this situation act out their frustrations. For example, it would be normal for them to assume some of their wives' housekeeping duties, but those men whose egos are most negatively affected will take a passive aggressive stance and do even less. That, in turn, will make their wives angry and the relationship can quickly go downhill.

What I would suggest in such situations is to arrive at some compromises that will offer him the most ego protection while still fulfilling the required duties. For example, perhaps instead of going to the supermarket, he could place orders by phone and wait for it to be delivered. Or go after working hours, even though he has the day free, just so as not to admit publicly that he is out of a job. His wife should accept such ruses without making snide comments, as long as the jobs get done. Hopefully, either he will find another job or get more used to his newfound status as house husband; but for the relationship not to suffer too badly, for a period it will be important to offer his ego as much protection as possible.

Now I don't want to imply that a woman who loses a job won't suffer. Of course she will, and there's a good chance that it will affect her libido as well. But since women tend to need comforting, it's likely that a woman who feels hurt may turn to her spouse's arms rather than turn aside. And since a woman doesn't have to be excited to engage in sex, she may decide that it's worth having sex just to get the consolation she needs, even if she doesn't have an orgasm. But if a man can't get an erection, then he's not going to want to engage in sex. And on top of that, if he does have erectile difficulties, the worries that this will happen again will probably become a self-fulfilling prophecy, making the situation that much worse. That's why many men will consider abstaining from sex if they're not in the mood rather than risk trying to make love and discovering that they can't.

They say that time heals all wounds and this is a case where I believe a little patience will pay off. But if it takes too long for a partner who has lost a job to pick him- or herself up, then consider going for some counseling. It may even be offered as part of a package that comes with that pink slip.

Losing a Friend or Relative

Another potential blow to a couple's love life can be losing a relative or close friend. While this can happen at any time in one's life, as we age, it does occur with greater frequency. Naturally the sadness that comes from such a loss is going to overcome your libido for a time, though after a period of mourning that should restore itself. But as well as mourning the loss of a loved one, or even someone not so loved, an older person will begin to feel the fragility of life. And the closer in age that the deceased was, the more severe will be the impact.

While you can never completely steel yourself against such occurrences—nor should you, as it is important to allow yourself to grieve for the passing of someone—what is important is how you react as a couple. You must be sensitive to the other person. If you feel that your partner is taking a particular death harder than might be expected, see if you can help. Don't allow your spouse to withdraw into a shell. Talk to him or her about the feelings he or she is having and offer as much comfort as you can.

The Whitewater Years are commonly a time when one or both of you might lose a parent. This is naturally a traumatic event and it is hard to predict how someone will react. Often long buried emotions get released, which may make a person extra sad, or actually bring some relief. Since you can't predict how you or your partner will react, you just have to read the signs and act accordingly.

And if you're the one feeling very blue, don't try to cover up these feelings. The more you bury them, the longer they will last and the more damage they can do. It is only by letting them out that you can overcome them, strange as that may seem.

And the saddest part about burying your feelings is that it also erases the happy memories. If you just stop thinking about a person who has died in order not to feel sad, then you also won't be able to enjoy remembering the happy moments. What normally happens is that after a while, the pain goes away and you can spend the rest of your life thinking about the good times you had with the person who has passed away. But if you adopt the course of being as stoic as possible and refusing to mourn, then you'll never graduate to that next phase. You'll never want to relive certain moments because you'll be afraid that such an experience will make you sad and that you'll give in to the grief you've been avoiding. So rather than stifle those tears, give in to them. In the long run, you'll be much better off.

Acting Your Age

Everyone has a hard time growing older. Most of the time you don't think about it, but when you do, it can be quite disconcerting. Psychologically you don't feel any different than when you were in your twenties, but every once in a while your body will remind you that your roaring twenties are long gone, and the psychological damage can be worse than the physical pain.

There are different ways of accommodating yourself to your age. Let me illustrate this with some personal experiences regarding skiing. I still love to go skiing. Now some people might tell me that at my age I ought to stop. And lots of people my age would stop. They say they wouldn't enjoy skiing as an old person and so they stay away from the slopes altogether. To me, that's nonsense. I don't ski for as many hours as I used to. I'm careful regarding conditions, and when they're not good, I don't leave the lodge. And I also afford myself the luxury of skiing with an instructor whose path I follow and who keeps an eye out that nobody runs into me. But I still go skiing and there are days I can say that I've never skied better. I would be foolish to give up something I enjoy just because I would refuse to make any accommodations to my age. So I do act my age on the slopes, but I also still ski.

The basic lesson here is that just because you may have to slow down in no way means that you have to stop, and that applies to anything, including sex. Making accommodations to how your body has changed is vital to growing older because that's how you continue to function. Since it becomes impossible to do all the things you once did, the alternative is to not do them at all. That's how you wind up a vegetable. So it's not a question of fighting your age or giving in to it, but adjusting to it.

This adjustment process is only beginning in your Whitewater Years, but because it is the beginning stage, it is a most important one. If you start out on the wrong foot, then you may never regain your balance.

Case History: Phil and Marilyn

Phil was an avid racquetball player. When he was fifty-four, he had a mild heart attack and required a pacemaker.

After his doctor told him it was alright to play racquetball again, he went back to his usual routine, which was to play for three hours on Saturday mornings. His wife, Marilyn, begged him to cut back, but he refused. She would be worried sick, and as the weekend approached, they would fight about how long he was going to play. One Saturday, Phil pulled his Achilles tendon while playing. It's a severe injury and at his age it meant that he would never play racquetball again. While Marilyn was relieved, Phil was actually upset at his wife, stubbornly blaming her for his injury instead of accepting the blame for pushing himself too hard.

It's possible that Phil would have torn his Achilles in any case, but at his age, he was definitely putting too much strain on his legs by playing for so long a time, and he was lucky that he didn't cause another heart attack. If he had agreed to cut back, he might have kept playing for many more years, but his stubbornness ended his playing days and also ended up damaging his relationship with his wife.

And while I'm on this topic, let me make one special plea that has to do with driving. As you get older, your reflexes slow down, your vision, particularly at night, worsens, and you just have to be more careful. You may have driven for years annoyed by older drivers who were "hogging" the road going slower than the rest of traffic, but at a certain age, speed really would be a killer. If you notice any weakening of your driving skills, please adjust and slow down. You won't only be making your own drives safer, but those of everybody around you too.

CHAPTER **11**

Better Health

THIS WAS A DIFFICULT CHAPTER FOR ME TO write. I enjoy giving people advice, but I really dislike having to scold people. We all know what it takes to maximize our health: eat right, stay away from addictive substances, get enough rest, exercise every day, and get regular checkups. Personally I would also add maintain a healthy relationship and enjoy a good sex life, but of course there are plenty of single people who are quite healthy, so that's just my bias. But then if we all know what we're supposed to do, how come so few of us actually follow these rules? I keep reading articles that say that 50 percent of us are overweight, so I don't need to be in the same room with you to guess that you're probably not in the best of shape. And more important, how can I get you to follow this simple set of rules without personally appearing on your doorstep every morning with a loudspeaker and a whip?

The answer is that I can't, but I do hope that I can offer you some suggestions that will at least get you on the right track.

You Don't Need to Be Perfect

The basic steps to good health are relatively uncomplicated, assuming you're already in fairly decent health, so the main obstacle is not physical but psychological. You could do everything necessary to maximize your health but you don't. In most cases this isn't an act of commission but rather one of omission. You think it's too hard and so you give up before even trying.

Case History: Eloise

The week before New Year's Day, Eloise drew up a list of how she was going to get herself into better health. She swore she'd stop smoking, get more exercise, and go on a strict diet. She had it all planned out and on New Year's Eve she ate as much as she could before the clock struck twelve, and then she stopped, cold turkey. She threw her cigarettes into the trash and stood as far away from the food table as possible. Those first few hours went very well, but the next morning her cravings for a cigarette were overwhelming, and since she hadn't thrown out the other packs she had in the house, she reached for one. At that point, she gave up on the entire plan.

One reason people give up so easily is that they set themselves up for failure, often in two ways. The goals they set are unreasonable, and as soon as they miss a goal, they decide the entire plan has been made valueless. To them it's like losing your virginity; once you've gone off your diet or had that one cigarette, there's no point in trying to begin all over again. But, of course, this is ridiculous. Your plan is one that is aimed at making changes over the remaining years of your life, so one little step backward doesn't mean that you should give up.

So the two first rules in drawing up a plan to improve your health is to set reasonable goals and not expect perfection. Following this rule, if losing weight is a goal, don't try to lose several pounds in one week, instead shoot for one or two pounds in a month. That way if you have an ice cream sundae that definitely is not on your diet, you won't have to give up the entire diet, but will just have to find ways of subsequently adjusting for those times you go off the plan.

I'm not telling you anything new here. But are there any factors that you have to consider now that you're in your Whitewater Years? The answer is yes. First of all, time isn't on your side. The mañana philosophy is no longer acceptable because you're closing in on an age where you're going to be facing new health problems, so the time to deal with the old ones has to be now, or never.

Another reason is that when you were in your youth, that is to say up until your Whitewater Years, your body's recuperative powers were good. They're now starting to weaken and you have to be proactive in order to bring them back into shape. For example, your bones are becoming less dense. I'm not talking about severe osteoporosis, just the normal aging process. This loss of bone density is why women as well as men shrink somewhat as they age (which is all that I needed considering I started out at 4' 7"!). But there is a way to make up for this. If you build your muscles, by training with weights, this added strength will compensate and help keep you upright. And the better your muscle tone, the less likely you are to be injured from slips or falls. But the time to begin this exercise process is now, not when you've already lost those inches.

As I've said several times, it is harder for a woman to lose weight after she's gone through menopause, but on the other hand, if she doesn't watch her weight, she will definitely gain pounds because her body is looking to add fat to make hormones. So suddenly women who never had a problem with their weight will find themselves avoiding the scales, afraid of the numbers they'll see.

And no longer having your kids at home may also help you to put on weight. Why is that you ask? There are a couple of reasons. The biggest, I'd guess, is that now that you're only two, you probably eat out more often. Visiting a restaurant is certainly less expensive as a couple than when you had teenagers at home, and it can be harder to cook for only two people, so you're drawn to letting someone else take care of this chore. And when faced with an entire menu of goodies, it's definitely harder to keep your calorie intake down. So eating out can be a downfall to a diet.

Let me offer a couple of suggestions regarding this potential trap. First of all, choose restaurants that don't have menus loaded down with high caloric meals, or at least have some items on their menus that are lower in fat and calories. My other tip is to adopt the philosophy that you don't have to clean your plate. I know that can be difficult considering that when the bill comes, you can see exactly what you're paying for that meal. One solution is to ask for a doggie bag, if there's enough to bother, but the other is to just ignore the cost and avoid those extra bites being mindful of what they would do to your waistline. As someone who went through two wars, I understand how hard this can be, but we're talking about your health here, so you have to overcome any natural instinct not to waste food.

Another factor that can lead to weight gain is that living in a household depleted of those who made the most dirt and mess, there's less housework to do. For people who's day job requires them to sit behind a desk all day, cleaning up may be their one activity that burns the most calories. So again, those missing children may result in additional pounds.

If you're not doing as much housework, then when you are home, that probably means you're sitting more. My suggestion is to make up for those cleaning duties by simply getting off your "you know what" more. For example, I always pace when I'm on the phone. Get yourself a portable phone and while you're talking, walk around the house. Or use a cell phone and go for a real walk outside while you're talking. And if you're watching television, pick up some small hand weights and move your arms. You'll develop tone and burn calories at the same time. In other words, don't sit still. They've done studies that show that fidgeters are skinnier, so even if all you do is fidget, it's better than sitting there like a lump.

Shop to Drop

Without all those empty stomachs to feed, you have to be very careful how you shop. Teens demand junk food, and even if you held them somewhat in check when they were around, there was more junk food around, and so more temptation for you. Now that they're out of the house, you have to be very careful not to fill your pantry with foods that are full of useless calories. If calorie-laden food is not within easy reach, you're likely to eat fewer calories. You can't snack on potato chips if there are none in the house. And conversely, if you're hungry and there's a bag of carrot sticks in the fridge and nothing else, you'll reach for those.

So one key to keeping your weight in check is to shop carefully. If you have a weight problem, you have to prepare for a trip to the supermarket as if you were going into battle. You must put together a list of items you need and then stick to it. Impulse buys tend to have the most calories, it seems. And the people who design supermarkets know this, which is why you'll usually find bars of candy right by the checkout counter. Another tip is to never go food shopping when you're hungry. If you're in a supermarket, surrounded by cookies and ice cream and other goodies and you're starving, your shopping basket will fill up to a much higher level than if you go right after you've had a decent meal. Actually, if your local supermarket takes orders by phone, then I would suggest that you use that method to do your shopping. That way you'll work from a prepared list and you won't come face to face with any tempting, calorie-laden delicacies.

Case History: Brett

Brett was fifty-three and owned a moving business, and while technically he wasn't a mover, when one of his men called in sick, Brett would fill in. His excuse was that if he burned a lot of calories lifting furniture, then he could eat to his fill that night, though he often ate to his fill on other nights as well. He wasn't very overweight, but he did have a pot belly. Then Brett went for a physical and his doctor told him that he had high cholesterol and that he had to be a lot more careful about what he ate. He tried to be careful for a few weeks, but he would grow angry looking at a menu and not being able to choose his favorite dishes, and despite his wife's warnings, he was soon back to his normal eating habits.

The Psychology of Dieting

Of course there are lots of people in their Whitewater Years who are forced to watch what they eat because their doctor reports that they have high cholesterol or high blood pressure or are borderline diabetic, and for the sake of their health, they have to cut back on how much they consume as well as be extra careful of what types of food they eat.

While you might think that getting that kind of bad news would kick you into high gear, let me warn you it doesn't always happen. Fear tactics often backfire. It's the "I dare you" syndrome from when you were a child. On your own you might never try to ride your bicycle without using your hands, but when your friends say, "I dare you," then you'll do exactly that. So when the doctor gives you an order, you might say to yourself, "Oh yeah, I can do whatever I want" and ignore those orders. Or it might not be the doctor that you're fighting, but the physical condition itself. Psychologically you might act like a teenager would when told to clean up his or her room, except here the enemy is not a scolding parent but your own body, the enemy within, so to speak.

Of course, this is one battle that you're ultimately going to lose. Either you follow orders or the condition will worsen and you'll be left with no choice. But to avoid these types of psychological battles with yourself to begin with, it is so much better if you get on this health-kick on your own before you get any bad news. If you take the initiative, you're in control. If you're not being forced into it, that will make it easier to bear. You can trick yourself into saying you like salads or that chocolate cake always makes you feel bloated a lot more easily than you can avoid those foods because you are being ordered to.

Rules of Exercise

The same psychological forces apply to exercise. Picture two individuals. One has been jogging for years. All the neighbors know this and barely wave when this person runs by. The other starts out for the first time and his neighbor shouts out a comment and this person has to answer, "My doctor told me to get more exercise." Is this second person likely to keep it up? No, because the act of exercise appears to be a punish-ment, exacted by the doctor or the physical condition or whatever. This person's natural reaction is to resent doing this form of exercise and to look for excuses to stop. But if you can start exercising before there's an actual dire need, then you're in control and psychologically it's much easier to keep going. You'll know that you're not giving in to some outside force, but that you're doing it out of your own volition. You'll feel good about it instead of getting negative feedback.

With exercise, as it was with dieting, it's important that you don't set goals for yourself that are ridiculously high. Don't say, "this time next year I'm going to run the marathon." The likely outcome is that it will soon become ap-parent that you don't have the time, desire, or willpower to train for a marathon, and then you're likely to give up jogging altogether. So it's much better to pick a reasonable goal that you're sure you can reach. And if you can't reach it one week, you mustn't give up but just start all over the next week as if nothing happened. But if it's a reasonable goal, then eventu-ally you'll be likely to hit it and can aim slightly higher.

There's another reason besides improving your health or losing weight that you should consider adopting an exercise regime, which while a bit sad, is a fact of life. Without a doubt, older adults face some age discrimination. That is certainly true in the business world. These days men and women in their fifties who lose their jobs are going to have a harder time finding new employment—at least at the same payscale they were at—than someone younger.

I'm not suggesting that you lie about your age on your ré-sumé. I've seen too many cases where people have altered their résumé only to be discovered and end up losing a job that they would actually have gotten if they'd told the truth. So while you can't change your actual age, you can make changes to improve your appearance. In today's job market, it is impor-tant that you appear as healthy and vital as possible. And that applies not only to someone who has lost a job and is looking for another one, but also to those who are employed. You want your bosses to look at you as someone who can handle his or her responsibilities and not as someone who might tire out. A pot belly, sagging shoulders, or a plodding walk will not project an image that will give management the confidence in you that you want them to have. But by keeping a high level of fitness, your appearance will improve. And also don't be afraid to let it be known that you exercise regularly, because that fact alone will make them look at you differently. But on the other hand, don't be a show-off. If you try to do too much and get injured, that will only make you seem fragile. So choose a moderate routine, at least to begin with.

Getting Enough Beauty Rest

While I'm on the subject of appearances, it certainly doesn't make you look good if you've got bags under your eyes and are constantly yawning. I understand that everybody doesn't need eight hours of sleep a night, but if you're getting significantly less than that, it's going to show. Here again, if this is a chronic condition for you, don't try to solve it on your own. If you've counted millions of sheep, then it's time to go to your doctor. I'm not talking about short intervals of insomnia. We all may develop that for a period of a week or two because of some problem we're dealing with that is making us nervous or worried. But if this continues over a longer period of time, rather than relying on over-the-counter remedies, seek professional help.

Kicking the Habit

One home remedy for sleeplessness that some people turn to is alcohol. I'm not against having a drink to relax you, but if you need to drink so much that you knock yourself unconscious, that's obviously not going to make you look and feel more alert the next day. You have a serious problem that needs attending to.

As anyone who abuses alcohol or smokes or takes drugs knows quite well, it's definitely very difficult to stop. So many people fail that you're to be forgiven if you can't do it on your own. But what you shouldn't be forgiven for is not seeking out some professional help. Sure you can try a variety of different ways to give up these bad habits on your own, but you shouldn't give up if you fail. There are programs that have a very high rate of success and you owe it to yourself and your spouse and the rest of your family, especially any current or future grandchildren, to take care of your health.

The fact that you don't have any children at home might make it easier. You're likely to be grumpy, to put it mildly, when trying to kick a habit, and so having children around could make it more complicated. Just make sure that your spouse understands exactly what you are doing so that he or she doesn't mistake your grumpiness as a personal affront. If you can work as a team, it will definitely make it easier, though the word *easy* is just not to be associated with such endeavors. But again, if you wait too long, it may become impossible, or if your body has become too severely damaged, then what's the point?

Getting Checked Out

As you near an age when something is more likely to break down, it becomes more and more important that you catch that "something" before it gets too bad. So while it's always important to go for a physical, it becomes vital starting in your Whitewater Years.

The need to encourage a visit to the doctor applies more to men than to women because it seems that we women never stop going to see the doctor, at least from the time we give birth, while many men avoid going like the plague. I suppose some men think it makes them seem weak. And while women are used to having their bodies probed, the check for prostate problems, which involves the doctor sticking his finger up the man's anus, is a test that many men would prefer to avoid.

While men should be able to get themselves in for a checkup on their own, to be realistic about it, in many households the wife is going to play an important role in getting this task accomplished. I know this may seem silly to you women, after all he's an adult, why should you have to treat him like a child? But if the alternative is that he doesn't get a checkup and winds up sick or worse, you're going to suffer terribly too. So while you may be in the right when you decide not to interfere, this could definitely be one of those situations where you're cutting off your nose to spite your face. I'm not saying that you have to be totally responsible for his health, after all, you certainly can't substitute your body to be examined, but if you need to be the one to make the appointment, then do it gladly rather than with a long face. You want him to get that exam, and getting into a fight over this issue is not going to make it anymore likely that he will go. Let's face it, you know how to cajole him when there's something you want, so put yourself into cajoling mode and help him to go for this exam, because in the larger scheme of things, there's nothing you want more than to have a healthy husband.

But as I indicated in previous chapters, just going to the doctor for an exam isn't enough. You have to tell the doctor what's wrong, so women, too, have to overcome their embarrassment when it comes to talking about sexual matters.

If you have pain during intercourse, or if you're not lubricating, or if your libido is at a very low level, speak up. That's the only way that you'll get the assistance you need.

And at this point, allow me to make one more pitch for mental health professionals. Our society doesn't look at mental health as being as important as physical health, and yet our mental health governs our physical health, to some degree, and mental health problems can definitely cause severe symptoms that make life go from difficult to hard to unbearable. If you feel that you, or your spouse, would benefit from seeing a professional counselor of some sort, don't hesitate to get that help. There's this image of the bearded psychiatrist who sees patients for decades that makes people believe that psychological counseling is not for them. But the vast majority of psychological counseling is short term. I, for example, am a behavioral therapist. I don't need to delve into your background. Yes, I need to know some things, but basically my aim is to change your future behavior. I can effectively help people in a matter of weeks, and there are many people in the mental health field who can do the same. So if you have a problem that requires the type of guidance that a mental health professional offers, seek it out. In the end, you'll be very glad you did.

CHAPTER **12**

Grandparents 'R Us

WHILE THERE EXISTS A STEREOTYPIC PICTURE of what grandparents are supposed to be like, these days that image seems to fit less and less. I'm sure when you picture the word *grandparent* you filter that image by thinking back on what your grandparents were like when you were a child. At that time of your life, when even teenagers seemed old, grandparents were downright ancient. And as you got older, they didn't get any younger. But since many grandparents are only in their forties, about the halfway mark of their entire life, they're anything but that older person who does nothing beyond baking cookies and sitting in a rocker.

Obviously some grandparents are old, but I don't want you to have any negative feelings about that moniker because whether you already enjoy the status of grandparent, or it's a milestone the future still holds for you, I want you to know there's no better role to play. Since nothing in our lives is perfect, there can be some rough spots, but I'm going to show you some tricks of the trade that will smooth them out. Overall, however, being a grandparent is the best job in the world.

If you are already a grandparent, especially if you are the first among your set of friends to reach that plateau, and you do feel that you are somehow diminished by this, then perhaps you'll draw some comfort in knowing that you are joining quite a fraternity/sorority. There are approximately ninety million grandparents in this country, and counting, so any stigma that many feel is attached to being labeled "grandma" or "grandpa" is being quickly overwhelmed by the sheer numbers of grandmas and grandpas out there. Being a grandparent is nothing to be ashamed of; quite the contrary, it's a status from which you should draw much pride.

Actually, throughout mankind's history, a grandparent was someone to be revered. So few people lived long enough to see their grandchildren that their immediate family deferred to them. Nowadays, there are many great grandparents around, and because of the way our culture worships youth, grandparenthood does not hold the value it once did. For example, there is a Grandparents Day, but it seems nobody celebrates it. That's sad, but to me, it doesn't matter what other people might think. I know how much satisfaction there is in being a grandmother, and so that's what I suggest you hold on to—the personal joy that comes from attaining this stage of life.

Does becoming a grandparent make the Whitewater Years any rougher? While it can, if you let it, and I'll get into that in a moment, I actually think the reverse is true. To me, grandchildren are the best stress-reducers there are. When you're with your grandchildren you can regress and act like a little child again. You're not the mommy or the daddy so discipline is not your concern. You're free to spoil your grandchildren all you want, or at least all that your children will let you. You don't have to put on any airs. You can totally relax when you're with them.

Of course all this assumes you're not one of those grandparents to whom the job of parenting has fallen. Being a grandparent who has been given the duties of raising a grand-child is a very stressful situation. I've actually written a book on grandparenting titled *Grandparenthood* in which I discuss that special situation in greater detail. I only mention it here because I do know that this occurs, more frequently than we'd like to admit, and I don't want to ignore this subset of grandparents, but they have their hands full whether they're in their Whitewater Years or at any other stage.

Schweigen, Schlucken, and *Schenken*

Under normal circumstances, meaning that if all the grandchil-dren are healthy, the only fly in the ointment that arises has to do with your grandchildren's parents, one of whom is your child. Now the best advice I can give you with their regard comes from my German background. It's a saying for grand-parents that goes *"schweigen, schlucken,* and *schenken,"* which translates as "keep your mouth shut, swallow, and give presents."

Let's start with the first piece of advice, keeping your mouth shut, as that's probably the most important one and also the hardest to follow. After a lifetime (your child's, not yours) of giving your child advice, it's not easy to pull up short and stop. As someone who gives advice all day long, believe me, I know how hard it is. But it's still something that you have to do. Now this doesn't apply to answering ques-tions. If you're asked for your advice, then you should ab-solutely give it. But if you're not, then you just have to keep quiet.

There are several good reasons for this. First of all, your child is 100 percent responsible for raising this child. When it needs to be fed at 2 A.M., crying because of a skinned knee, or needs help with homework, it's the parent's responsibility.

CONQUERING THE RAPIDS OF LIFE

So your advice on some small, specific matter is like a drop in the ocean. Your child is responsible for the bottom line and so he or she must make those decisions, just like you made them when you were doing the parenting.

The other reason is that your child isn't the only person bringing up this child (at least hopefully not). There's another parent, and the two of them are going to get into some parenting disagreements as it is. Throwing another person into the mix (actually, potentially, another four people) is not going to be helpful but will only confuse the situation. That's right, you're not the only grandparent, so if it were okay for you to put your two cents in, then it would be okay for the other three to do the same.

And what if you know that there's another grandparent butting in all the time? Here's a case where two wrongs definitely don't make a right. And believe me, the parents of the child will appreciate your silence and you'll end up getting to spend more quality time with your grandchild than if you become another source of unwanted advice.

Case History: Grandma Agnes

Grandma Agnes was flying in to spend the weekend at her daughter-in-law's house. She was delighted because she'd get to spend a lot of time with her eighteen-month-old grandson Peter. She hadn't seen Peter in three months and she couldn't believe how much he had changed. The first few hours were fabulous, but then it was time for Peter to take his nap and her daughter-in-law opened up her blouse and started to nurse him. Grandma Agnes was aghast. She thought that at eighteen months Peter should have long ago been weaned off the breast. Not only was she aghast, but she stated her opinion quite assertively. Her daughter-in-law was not about to give in, and a bit of a fight ensued. A coolness descended between the two women that permeated the weekend and made what should have been an enjoyable time miserable for everyone and boded ill for future visits as well.

The second piece of advice, swallow, is actually similar to the first; sort of reinforcing it. Some advice is given proactively, perhaps starting before this grandchild is even born. That all falls under the first category. But what if you're with the child and its parents and a situation arises of which you don't approve? Do you blurt out your feelings or do you swallow them? Looking at the damage that can be done from the case history above, hopefully you'll see the benefits of swallowing them.

What often happens is that the grandparent with a complaint (or set of grandparents, as the couple will often huddle together at home and discuss endlessly the fate of their poor, mistreated grandchild) will talk to the parent who is their child. That does make it easier as your child at least has to listen to you, but you should never assume that what you say to that child doesn't get repeated to his or her spouse. Don't you and your spouse always talk about everything? Then the same will hold true for them. So you can get into just as much trouble by speaking to one parent as two.

Now let me be clear here. If by some chance your grandchild is actually being abused, then you must speak up. But if it's a question of how that child is being raised, no matter how strongly you disagree, my advice is to keep those thoughts to yourself. The reason: the parents are unlikely to listen to you and so all that you'll accomplish is to drive a wedge between you and your grown child and then you'll end up seeing less of your grandchildren. So while it may be difficult for you to swallow those words, that's what you must do in order to keep the peace and maximize the pleasure you get out of having grandchildren.

Gift Giving

Now for that final piece of advice, giving gifts. There are two types of gifts that you can offer. Some are items that the child will enjoy—toys, chocolates, fancy clothes when they get older—and the other group are items that the parents would have to buy for the child anyway—like everyday clothes or a new winter coat or a computer—and that you'll be saving them money by buying yourself. Obviously your own economic circumstances will dictate how much of this you can do, and as soon as the child is old enough to realize that grandma and grandpa can be a source of desired items, then you'll want to concentrate on those. Are you buying the child's love? Not exactly, but let's face it, grandparents aren't necessarily the most exciting people to a child, especially to a grandchild who is old enough to go out to play with friends. So if your visit comes with a small bribe, well, I think it's a fair exchange. Younger children, say under two, don't really need such gifts, apart from maybe a tasty treat, and since the parents of a young child may be in need of financial help, your gifts at that stage can be of the more utilitarian type.

Case History: Grandpa Jeff

Grandpa Jeff lived only a few blocks away from where his son, daughter-in-law, and grandchildren, four-year-old Karen and six-year-old Jack, lived. He was a widower and on summer nights, after eating an early supper, he would walk over to their house, stopping by a candy store to buy something for the children. He would show up at about 6 P.M., candy in hand, and since the kids knew he was coming, they'd be waiting for him. His daughter-in-law really loved Jeff, but she didn't want her children eating candy before dinner. She'd tried to tell him, but he didn't want to disappoint the kids and so he ignored her pleas.

Of course, while gift-giving is a great way to bond with your grandchildren, any gift does have to have the parents' blessings. Giving candy before dinner is a problem not only because it spoils the children's appetite, but also because it undercuts the mother's authority. (I even heard of one set of grandparents who would wake the children in order to give them candy!) If she doesn't want her children having candy before dinner, then it's her right to enforce this ban. To insist is only going to cause problems down the road, and there is usually an acceptable solution that can be arrived at if you're both willing to compromise. For example, in the case of Grandpa Jeff, Mom could have kept the candy until after dinner, or he could have brought something else. Or he could buy a large bag of marbles and every day bring a couple of them over for each child. Or simply present them each with a shiny new quarter. (That there will soon be quarters from every state can make them even more interesting to collect.) Or he could help them start a coin or a stamp collection, bringing a new one every day.

And if you have a problem deciding what to give, then consult with the parents. They know the child best and can assess what they might need and want. It can be fun trying to think of the perfect gift, but if it turns out that they already have it, then that's going to ruin the pleasure.

When to Spoil

Now this rule of not getting in between the children and their parents is meant for every area, not just gift-giving. If your grandchildren know that they can come to you to get their way on things like bedtime, watching television, doing homework, and so forth, then they'll do it again and again. This will create bad feelings between you and their parents and in the long run will only cause you problems. So, yes, you should be able to spoil them, but just do it moderately and in areas where their parents give you the okay.

Maintaining Communications

With everyone being so busy these days, at all age levels, it can be difficult to maintain communications with your grandchildren. If you're both working and they're going to school and spending time with their friends, how do you integrate yourselves into their lives? The obvious answer is to use the many new means of communications that are now available, like e-mail and Instant Messaging and cell phones. But that only works if you have something to communicate about. If you haven't experienced it, we've all seen the scenario where an adult asks a child a few questions, gets some one-word answers in return, and the conversation ends as the child goes off to play video games.

It takes some planning to avoid this type of noninteraction. Instead of just asking questions, you should prepare for such visits. I'm not saying every time, but enough times that your grandchildren will know to expect the occasional surprise and so will always look forward to seeing you. (This is harder to do if you see them quite often, but still a worthwhile exercise.) Here are some suggestions of what I'm talking about:

- Bring along a family photo album and look at old pictures with them, and tell them some tales that go with them so that they can get a sense of their family's history.
- Explore your heritage. If, for instance, you're Italian, cook them an Italian meal; look at a map of Italy, highlighting

where the family comes from; teach them some Italian words.

- If your grandchildren like sports, go over a famous year of a team you both like, such as a year when the baseball team you root for went to the World Series. You'd have to do some homework, but it would be a fun way to spend time together.
- Write a story or poem together.
- Teach them how to cook a simple dish.

I'm sure you can think of many other things to do with your grandchildren, but very often these activities will take some preparation, so you can't expect to succeed if you wait until the last minute.

When Grandchildren Visit

When you had little children, you were used to the mess they make. Stepping over toys became second nature and crumbs under the dining table weren't a big deal. If you haven't had young children living with you for a while, you've probably developed new habits. Your house is much neater and since you can keep it that way, it's become important to you that it stays that way. But, of course, that doesn't work if a new set of children arrives—your grandchildren.

Most pleasurable activities require some compromises. If you go skiing, your nose is going to get cold and you'll get snow down into your boots. If you play a sport, you'll get sweaty. If you eat lobster, you'll need a bib. And if your grandchildren come over, you're going to have to give up some of your neatness. Kids don't make deep messes that take a long time to clean up, unless you serve them chocolate pudding on the living room couch, and then you're asking for trouble. It may take twenty minutes or half an hour to clean up after they're gone, and you'll enjoy the experience of having them over a whole lot more if you just learn to accept the mess and deal with it afterward. They're too adorable and too much fun to allow yourself to get grumpy. It's their free spirit that makes them fun to be with so don't try to squelch it; in the long run you'll be hurting yourself more by missing out on getting "down and dirty" with them.

How Grandchildren Impact Your Relationship

Obviously I'm a great fan of grandchildren, and while I wouldn't want to exaggerate their powers, just the way I said that they can be great stress relievers, they can also have a very strong impact on your marriage relationship.

One of the things I said in an earlier chapter is that you should do things together, like share a hobby. This can be easier said than done. For example, if he likes to play golf and she doesn't, and he already spends a lot of his free time on the course, then there won't be that much free time to go, for example, antiquing. You should find ways of overcoming such obstacles, but while you're doing that, you can already discover the ways in which grandchildren can help to bring you together. I know I shouldn't be comparing grandchildren to a hobby, as they're much more important than that, but they can share many of the qualities of a hobby. If they help you to relax when you're in their presence, if they are a topic of conversation between you and your spouse, if they give you pleasure just thinking about them, then they obviously have great powers. And among those powers is the ability to heal any rifts that have developed between you and your spouse.

Remember what I was saying about empty-nest syndrome. Many couples find that after their children have left home, they don't have enough to talk about to sustain the relationship. Well, grandchildren can definitely help to bridge that gap. I don't believe that you should substitute your grandchildren for your children, so that they're the only things holding up your relationship. But if they permit you to begin the process of getting back together, then they've served an important purpose.

And again, if you've become set in your ways, and those ways are in a parallel universe with that of your spouse, then by allowing your grandchildren to break these patterns, you can, perhaps, interact with your spouse more often. But such interactions won't serve to heal your relationship unless you make the most of them. If you're pleasant in front of them but then go back to scowling at each other when you return home, the visit won't have served much purpose. But if you take advantage of the goodwill that is in the air and make an effort to get a little closer each time you are with your grandchildren, then the rift can be healed. Here are some hints of how you can do this:

- Instead of preparing Sunday dinner for your children and grandchildren, go to visit with them for a few hours and then go out for dinner together. If the atmosphere is a positive one, during this time alone together, perhaps you can get a little closer.
- Borrow grandchildren for a time. Maybe while you're showing them the zoo, you can hold hands or put your arms around each other.
- Work on a project together involving your grandchildren. Let's say that you want to get them into stamp collecting, then work on buying them stamps together, so that it becomes your hobby as well.

- Start a grandparents' club with some of your friends. By getting together with friends (i.e., socializing together), you'll find that the stimulation will bring the two of you closer together as well.

A Special Word about Grandmothers

Women who work outside of the home, and continue to do so in their Whitewater Years, definitely feel that they have a valuable contribution to make to society. But women who are not employed, whether or not they ever were, and whose children have flown the coop may feel that they do not serve a useful purpose, and such feelings can lead to depression and other problems. Another reason that women are more prone to such feelings is that while a man can potentially father a child into his old age, once a woman has passed menopause, that is not in the cards. So not only has she lost her need to mother, but even her actual ability to once again become a mother.

But just because she no longer can bear children does not mean that she is finished being a useful human being, by any means. In fact, I read about a fascinating study that found that throughout history, grandmothers, and maternal grandmothers in particular, played such an important role that it meant life or death for their grandchildren. In other words, child mortality rates are lower when there is a grandmother around than if there is not one. So you see that grandmothers are a very valuable asset.

Now I admit that such life-or-death scenarios apply mainly to primitive societies where everyone is hanging on to life by the skin of their teeth and so every little bit of assistance can be of tremendous importance. But while having a grandmother around may not have life and death consequences for children in a modern society, they still have an important role to play.

Put an End to Paternal Grandparents Discrimination

You may have noticed that I said the research showed that the maternal grandmother was the important one. As it turns out, maternal grandmothers remain more important today too, as mothers—who retain the greater portion of childcare even these days—are more likely to turn to their own mothers for help, whose aid they have always had, than to the mothers of their spouses.

But this "discrimination" doesn't have to continue. These studies have shown that both sets of grandparents want to take part, so it is up to you, if you are the paternal grandparents, to step up to the plate. Just because your daughter-in-law may be reluctant to ask you for help doesn't mean that she'll reject your help if you offer it. And that applies to grandparents of both sexes. You might have to be a bit more circumspect when helping out than maternal grandparents, at least in the beginning. But once you've established the right rapport, soon thereafter there will be no distinguishing between the two sets of grandparents and you can contribute as often and as much as you want.

Healthy Grandparenting

If grandchildren were to serve no other purpose, you should certainly use them as an inducement to take care of your health. I've dealt with health in earlier chapters, but if you're still putting off getting the proper treatment for some medical condition or another, the concept that this disease would either limit or cut short the time you could spend with your grandchildren should, I hope, be enough of an incentive to get you to make an appointment with your doctor.

If, for example, you're a woman with a constant urge to urinate who has put off going to the doctor, as soon as you've spent some time staring at a new grandchild, your first call should be to take care of this problem. You wouldn't want to miss being able to take your grandchild for a walk in the park, for example, just because of a bladder problem for which there's a remedy. And there are plenty of milestones ahead for this grandchild, and potential other grandchildren as well, that you could be there to see, but only if you take care of yourself.

Grandchildren as Financial Advisors

The sight of a grandchild, or a room full of them, can also make you start thinking of their future financial needs. If you've got money that you would like to be able to leave to them, there may be financial arrangements that have to be made sooner rather than later. So let your accountant know of your new status and see whether or not there are financial moves that you should be making.

The Favorite

One sticky situation that can arise is when a particular grandchild ends up being the favorite. Sometimes both grandparents will have the same favorite and sometimes not. On the one hand, you can't help your feelings. Perhaps it's the first grandchild that sticks out as being special. Or maybe you end up bonding with one that is of the same sex as you. Whatever the reason, if you have a favorite, there's nothing you can do about it, except to not let it be known. Favoritism is something that you have to feel in your heart, not show outwardly. Now it's possible that the favorite will know, or that any you don't favor will also guess your feelings. It just may not be something that you can hide all that easily. But when it comes to giving gifts, or hugs, or talking on the phone, or whatever, then you absolutely must show equality. (I'm talking when they're little, of course. If you have a teenage grandchild who's covered with tattoos and studs, then you have every right to let that one know that you don't approve and that he or she is not your favorite.)

Some spouses argue over favoritism. If your spouse is letting you know that you're showing your favoritism too openly, then they're actually doing you a favor, and rather than argue back, you should thank them. But if your spouse knows you have a favorite and that you're trying hard not to show it, then they should leave you alone. Your grandchildren aren't identical and they each have different qualities that you love. If one has more, so be it. So if you're making a concerted effort not to play favorites, your inner feelings on this issue are not something that needs to be examined under a microscope. Your spouse can help keep you in line, but should not cross the line when it comes to watching over how you respond to your grandchildren.

Conclusion

THERE'S A DISTINCT ENERGY THAT EMANATES from the streets of New York, and if you were to walk around New York's Times Square, the heart of The Big Apple, you'd find it filled with tourists from all over the world with rapt expressions as they try to absorb as much of it as they can.

You can see the same expressions on the faces of people skiing down a snow-covered slope, repelling down a mountainside, digging for a ball on a tennis court, or, of course, paddling furiously down some rapids in a kayak.

People everywhere make elaborate plans and spend enormous sums in order to add some excitement to their lives. But if you're either on the threshold of or actually in your Whitewater Years, you're going to get excitement aplenty without having to do a thing to get it started, besides having a birthday or two.

I'm not being facetious here. I believe the Whitewater Years comprise an important period in everyone's life. The changes that will occur will make it a somewhat rocky ride, but how much you get out of the experience will depend on your attitude. This is one of those occasions when you could look at the glass as being half-empty or half-full. As you may have guessed by now, I'm a half-full type of woman, and I hope that now that you've just about finished reading this book that you're ready to join me in this outlook. Because if you can adopt a positive view, then I think you'll find the Whitewater Years an exciting period of your life. But if you persist on looking at each change that you encounter as a problem, then you could just as easily have a miserable time of it.

The Energy Bunny

I'm constantly being asked by people how I maintain such a high energy level and positive outlook on life. If I had a dollar for each time someone said I'd be a millionaire if I could package this energy and joie de vivre, I would be a millionaire. Now I have no idea how to bottle enthusiasm, but I can certainly tell you how to make your outlook as positive as possible.

I've had a private practice for over twenty years, specializing in sex and marital therapy. I don't practice psychology per se but rather what is called *behavioral therapy*. I don't go digging into a person's past to find out what makes him or her tick. I give my clients exercises to get them going in a new and more positive direction. This type of therapy suits me to a tee because it's how I operate.

Looking at my life objectively, I could have a lot to complain about. I was orphaned at the age of ten. At the Swiss school I was sent to, they didn't teach the girls reading, writing, and arithmetic, only how to be housemaids. I stopped growing at 4' 7". I was severely wounded in Palestine. I came to the United States a single mother, and my first job was as a cleaning lady.

You Can't Forget

While I could have spent my days complaining about all these negative events, I didn't. I certainly never forgot them, and I continue to feel considerable pain when I think back on that horrible day when I last saw my family. I don't advocate senility as a cure for anything. I don't want to forget a single moment of my life. But remembering is not the same as dwelling upon. I give myself a few minutes to remember, and then I'm off doing new things, full throttle. And that's what I tell the people who come to my office to do. You can't forget what has happened to you, but you also can't allow it to hold you back.

Let's look at a specific example. You're faced with a case of empty-nest syndrome. Your children have left the house, and the two of you feel awkward around each other. You're not delighted to see the other one's face when you get home in the evening, so you try to minimize the time you spend with your spouse, slinking off into the den or the basement at the first opportunity. You tolerate each other at meal times, and you share the same bed, and maybe even have sex once in a while, but, as they say, the thrill is gone.

Faced with such a bleak situation, no one could fault you for looking back and trying to see what went wrong. But would such an assessment get you anywhere? Probably not. What's done is done. You could find a hundred things you should have done twenty years ago, but you didn't. The only question that remains is: what can you do now to right this situation, if anything?

There's no one thing, of course. It's not as if you have appendicitis and surgery will cure the problem. If the relationship can be fixed, it will take a series of steps. So what you have to do is take the first one. That could be as simple as making plans to go out to dinner. When you're at dinner, put every ounce of effort you have into making it pleasant and enjoyable. If you both end the evening feeling good, then you know that with more effort and energy you can put your relationship on the right track. Focus on the future and do everything you can to get there, starting right this very second.

Getting Out of the Woods

If you're lost in the woods, the worst thing you can do is to wander around in circles. You have to use the sun to make sure that whatever direction you're going in, it's a direction and not a circular path. Eventually you'll reach something. In the case of a relationship, that something might be the realization that it can't be fixed. If that's the case, then you have to move on with your life alone. But at least you'll be moving on. At least you'll be getting somewhere. Eventually you won't be lost.

It's perfectly okay to make mistakes. We all do, and you can be sure we'll all make more of them. But you can't allow those mistakes to freeze you like a deer caught in the headlights. You do the best you can to correct the mistake and you move on, not allowing the potential for making another mistake stop you from encountering success. If you keep plodding forward, and if you also keep your eyes open, peeled for any opportunities to grab, then you will find those opportunities and you will succeed.

You might not succeed in the way you had originally planned. I never dreamed of one day becoming the celebrated Dr. Ruth. Having the spotlight turned on me wasn't just the furthest thing in my mind; it wasn't on my mind at all. But the element of surprise wasn't going to stand in my way either. Life hits you with bad things, and it also hits you with good things. You have to make the most of all of them.

It's Not Having More Energy,
It's Managing Your Time

So let's go back to that question of where I find all my energy. Do I have any more energy than you do? The real answer is no. What I have is a philosophy that doesn't permit me to say to myself, "Ruth you're too tired to do that." If I'm invited to a party, I go because there's no telling whom I'm going to meet there. If there are two parties, I'll try to go to both of them. If it's a choice between going out and staying home, I'll always go out.

Obviously you shouldn't bite off more than you can chew. For example, I give lectures all around the globe and these take up a lot of time. I was recently offered the opportunity to teach courses both at Princeton and at Yale. That's something I always wanted to do, but I knew that I couldn't travel constantly and give these courses, so I cut out the traveling. Or let's say, I cut down. But this decision to cut back was made so that I could teach courses at two of the most prestigious universities in the land, not to sit like a blob watching television. My minister of communications, Pierre Lehu, who helped me write this book, has a wife who from time to time runs for public office. It requires hundreds of dogged hours of work, and she doesn't necessarily win anything because of all that effort. But even after losing an election, she's better off than the person who would like to be in a position of leadership, but who gives up without ever trying.

Find a Goal

You can find the energy if you have a goal. If you had to work fifteen hours a day just to feed your family, you'd do it. It wouldn't be a question of finding the energy, right? If you don't need to work that hard to put food on the table and pay the rent, instead of wasting those extra hours, which are so very precious, then find another goal. Maybe some people will shake their heads at you. They'll say to themselves, why is that person working so hard? But at the end of the day, and more important, at the end of your life, you'll be glad you put in those extra hours doing something interesting rather than having wasted hundreds of hours being bored.

You are given very few hours on this earth, maybe even fewer than you think. Wasting them is the worst thing you can do. Using each one up to the very last second is the best. Of course you can't use all twenty-four of the ones you're allotted daily. You have to sleep and eat, and so forth. And if you work, then large chunks of hours are taken from you. So when you analyze it, you really don't have a lot of free hours left. So spending them doing something unproductive is really terrible. Ask yourself this question, and give yourself an honest answer: how often do you turn off the television feeling satisfied? Another way of putting that is, how many hours do you waste sitting in front of it vegging out? If someone forced you to be a vegetable you'd be horrified, and yet here you are voluntarily putting yourself into such a state, night after night.

If you're very tired, lie down, set the alarm, and take a thirty-minute nap. When you get up, your energy will be restored and you can do something active. Better to rest constructively and utilize the rest of the evening than waste all of it doing basically nothing.

So you see, having energy is more a case of proper time management than anything else. If you have the motivation, you can always find the time because during the course of a day, there are always minutes that would otherwise be wasted.

Creating Energy

There's another benefit of being active and that is that it allows you to be more active. When you're sitting around, your energy level actually goes down. You don't have more energy after slouching on the couch for ten minutes staring into space; you have less. So if you're serious about increasing your level of energy, what you have to do is increase your level of activity. The more you do, the less tired you'll feel, and the more you'll accomplish.

This advice is important to someone of any age, but it's more important to someone in his or her Whitewater Years. If you waste time as a youth, there's always the chance that you can catch up. But if you waste time in your Whitewater Years, you may never get that second chance. In fact, this may be your second chance! I started my new life as Dr. Ruth when I was in my fifties and I'm the first to admit that it would have been much harder had this opportunity presented itself at a later age. I'm not saying it would have been impossible, just harder. And the fact that my children were grown and I was at that time only responsible to myself actually made it easier than it might have been a few years earlier. (It may not have been easier on my late husband, but the fact is that he was busy taking advantage of his Whitewater Years as well, getting an M.B.A. and taking the piano lessons he'd always wanted.)

The Bottom Line

So what's the bottom line? As you enter your Whitewater Years you have to be aware that your lifestyle is going to undergo some changes. You can't look at this in a negative way, but instead you must try to pull as many positives out of this time of your life as possible. You have to make all the improvements that you can while you can so that when you enter the next phase of your life you're as well prepared as you can be. You have to take care of your health, which will mean spending more time with doctors. You have to get more exercise. You have to develop new interests. You have to repair any damage to your relationship.

If you do a good job, you can make your senior years a time to thrive. If you're lax, then your last decades could be spent miserably. Remember, the Whitewater Years are a transitional stage. Like any set of rapids, they don't last for long. Your voyage will continue but the conditions will be different. And it's how well you handle the Whitewater Years that will determine those conditions.

There's a saying "the best is yet to come." In the case of your life, I think that philosophy can be counterproductive. It's possible that you've already had your best years. But that doesn't mean that your future doesn't hold a lot of wonderful days in store for you. As the great baseball legend Satchel Paige said: "Don't look back, something might be gaining on you." He continued to play professional baseball until he was almost sixty (or maybe even older, as his birthday was more a matter of conjecture than fact). He also said: "Age is a question of mind over matter. If you don't mind, it doesn't matter."

If you have the right philosophy about aging, you, too, can keep experiencing life at its fullest. So don't look at those rapids with fear, but rather with excitement. You will survive this test, but if you have the right attitude, you will enjoy it, too, and come out of it ready for whatever else life has in store for you.

Index

acting your age, 195–97

activities, 111–12, 139–40; damaged relationship and, 172–73; romance and, 143–45; sharing, 37–38. *See also* exercise

admitting problem, xiv, xvi

advertising, 176

aerobic exercise, 94–95

affairs. *See* extramarital affairs

afterplay, 76–77

age brackets, 2–3

alcohol, 102–3, 186–89, 207–8

Alzheimer's, 28

anger, 15–16

anoxia, 66

anxiety, 12–13

appearance: depression and, 58; job market and, 206–7; men and, 93–94; men's sexuality and, 81–82; women and, 52–55

arteries, hardening of, 87, 95

arthritis, 51–52, 60; men and, 91–92, 98

The Art of Arousal (Westheimer), 185

attitude, 71, 138, 139, 227–28, 234. *See also* positive thinking

baby boom generation, 130–31

behavioral therapy, xiii–xiv, 210, 228

benign prostatic hypertrophy (BPH), 90

bladder, overactive, xiv, xv, 43–46, 224

blood flow to penis, 66–67, 86–87, 98, 168

blood pressure, 44, 56–57, 87

bone density, 28, 201

boredom, 109–10, 150

BPH. *See* benign prostatic hypertrophy

breast cancer, 31, 52–54

INDEX

diabetes, 44, 72, 87, 95
diet, 37, 202
dieting, 204–5
Ditropan XL, 45
divorce, 105–7, 165–66
driving, 197

ejaculation, 70–72, 97, 170, 183
elderly parents, 4–5, 132–34; guilt feelings, 137–38; learning to adjust, 134–36; romance and, 160–61
Elmiron, 47
embarrassment, xiv, 44–46, 84–85
empty-nest syndrome, xv, 123, 229; activities, 111–12; alcohol and, 102–3; boredom, 109–10; case histories, 102–3, 108–9, 117; communication, 119–20; counseling and, 102, 115–18; cures for, 107–9; damaged relationship, 102–5, 114; decision making, 105–7; departure of children, xiii, 8, 10, 60; extramarital affairs and, 171; getting out of house, 110, 111, 120; grandparents and, 221; grieving period, 101–2; individuality and, 120–21; intellectual pursuits, 113–14; other couples and, 112, 113, 114; self-help suggestions, 118–20

endometrial cancer, 31
energy, 228, 231, 232, 233
enthusiasm, 228
erectile dysfunction, 70; blood flow and, 86–87; injections for, 72–73, 82, 89; job loss and, 193–94; medications and, 88; psychological issues, 80–81, 90
erection, 7–9, 16; partner's role, 168–69; psychogenic, 64–68, 167–68
estate planning, 140
estrogen, 27, 31, 37
exercise, 137, 172; men and, 94–95, 96; for penis, 66–67; romance and, 155–56; rules of, 205–7; sex as form of, 97; weight training, 201, 203; women and, 31, 36–37. *See also* activities
extramarital affairs, 106, 165–66; case histories, 166–67, 174–75, 179–80; counseling, 178–79; male issues, 170–72; men's reasons for having, 167–72; oral sex and, 169–70; women's reasons for having, 174–78.

fantasy, 158–59
fat cells, 37
fear, 99–100, 140
financial issues, 131, 189–90, 224

About the Authors

Dr. Ruth K. Westheimer is a psychosexual therapist who helped to pioneer the field of media psychology. Her media career began on radio in 1980 with "Sexually Speaking," a program that was soon syndicated across the country. She has hosted numerous television programs, including *The Dr. Ruth Show* and *Ask Dr. Ruth*. She has also appeared on almost every national talk show, including *The Today Show*, *The Tonight Show*, *David Letterman*, and *Conan O'Brien*. Her syndicated newspaper column circles the globe, and she has been featured in almost every major magazine, including on the covers of *People* and *TV Guide*.

Currently Dr. Westheimer is an adjunct professor at New York University and is teaching courses at Princeton in the spring of 2003 and at Yale in 2004. She also taught at Lehman College, Brooklyn College, Adelphi University, Columbia University, and West Point. She is a Fellow of the New York Academy of Medicine and has her own private practice. She frequently lectures at universities across the country and has twice been named College Lecturer of the Year. She has lectured at more than two hundred college campuses including Harvard, MIT, Princeton, Columbia, Brown, Notre Dame, UCLA, UNC, Johns Hopkins, Georgia

Tech, Texas A&M, USC, and Trinity College. She is the author of twenty-three books, including *Sex for Dummies*, *Power: The Ultimate Aphrodisiac*, and *Grandparenthood*. She has her own website on AOL (www.drruth.com). Dr. Westheimer resides in Manhattan and has two children and four grandchildren.

Pierre A. Lehu has been Dr. Westheimer's "Minister of Communications" for the past twenty-two years. He is the co-author of *Dr. Ruth's Guide to College Life*, *Dr. Ruth Talks about Grandparents*, and *Rekindling Romance for Dummies*. A graduate of New York University (B.A. and M.B.A.), he resides in Brooklyn and is married with two children, one attending graduate school and the other college.